"THE MISSING PUZZLE PIECE"

BY: ROBERT T. ADCOCK

Copyright © 2020 by Robert T. Adcock

All rights reserved. This book or any portion thereof may not be reproduced or transmitted in any form or mr, electronic or mechanical, including photocopying, recording, or by any information storage or retrieval system, without the express written permission of the copyright owner except for the use of brief quotations in a book review or other noncommercial uses permitted by copyright law.

Printed in the United States of America

Library of Congress Control Number:		2020908993
ISBN:	Softcover	978-1-64908-187-2
	eBook	978-1-64908-186-5

Republished by: PageTurner Press and Media LLC
Publication Date: 5/13/2020

To order copies of this book, contact:
PageTurner Press and Media
Phone: 1-888-447-9651
order@pageturner.us
www.pageturner.us

TABLE OF CONTENTS

Preface: vii

Chapter 1: "Embark on the Journey" 1

Chapter 2: "The Oldest Religion" 12

Chapter 3: "The Expansion Of The East" 18

Chapter 4: "The Movement Westward" 25

Chapter 5: "The Banish One" 36

Chapter 6: "The Prodigal Son" 42

Chapter 7: "The Unholy" 49

Chapter 8: "The Miscellaneous Ones" 54

Chapter 9: "The Final Piece of the Puzzle" 61

Preface:

This is not to change your thoughts or your admiration to your religion. This is merely to educate and instruct people. The book will cause some stir in one's soul is probably an understatement. The reason for this idea some people might think that I'm a lunatic, or that I'm trying to commit heresy on a massive global scale. This is not my intent to do what so ever. This book will provide the foundation and the understanding if you allow it. I'm not trying to brain wash people like I said before its intent is to educate the soul so you can open your spirit up and listen to what is going on around you. People from all parts of the world, in general, have a natural state that is to be good hearted, however, it is a select few that cause the most damage to the world. Society and individuals do want to live in peace, however, those select few throughout time have embedded thoughts and ideas that have been pass down from generation to generation to fuel the fire of hate and ignorance. This book might not reach all the people who read it but I hope I can touch at least one person. Now, religion is a fickle mistress and can be summed up from one aspect to another. All religion is built on the predapiss of good will and honest living. The patriarch of a religion is to keep the masses from getting out of hand to ordained control so that society doesn't cavitate into anarchy. This is a caveat without some kind of structure the race of our society as we know it would be on the brink of an animalistic rule. In essence, religion has save ourselves from ourselves. This is a good thing like all checks and balance in life to much of control without guidance is bound to end up in disaster. However, in this book, this is what I will be talking about the apex and the decline of religion across the world, and the pieces that it has left behind to where we became blind and cannot see what is right in front of us. So, while reading this book I implore you to keep an open and optimistic mind to the notion that maybe there is more to our belief then what we practice today. Sometimes in our path to seek the truly wisdom of peace and tranquility, hoping that all of mankind can arrive on the same page, we lose sight on the voyage when we first had started out. I hope that by reading this we can find our way back from the brink of destruction and continue down the path that we were meant to go down. So, upon after reading this whatever outcome you deride from, I hope it is to your satisfaction.

Chapter 1:

"Embark on the Journey"

We could start from the beginning or we could start at the end, but let us start in the middle and build to our conclusion like looking at a nautilus. Since the dawn of mankind, we have been wondering why are we here and where are we moving to? Our nature as homo- sapiens; we are explorers, thinkers, hunters, gathers, and builders. I am a man of science as well as religion, I come to you as a humble man in hopes you can understand where am I coming from. What I'm asking is not an easy task it will require a lot of patience and understanding that will lead to some insight on what you may have or may not have known, that I have come across in my life's journey. I will be using my life situations and religion as well as scientific explanations to give you that parallel divine thought.

In this era, we have technology that is unfathomable that we use on a daily basis. Every day we grow and the abilities of our nature grow with us. The output of data streams, binary bits, and algorithms surpasses what our forefathers have written in books, manuscripts & scrolls. The reason that I'm starting out like this is so you can nibble on the cusp of knowledge if you will. I will be drawing conclusions based on facts and understandings of the different time eras. To show how things were done in a way of life and thinking, and at the same time asking questions that you may have and I as well, while maintaining the true nature of this journey.

Now, what is time; I mean what is time exactly, is it a unit of measurement that we see by looking at a watch, or by the way how we see the seasons change, or is it the understanding on how we follow in the footsteps of our religion? Is time the antiquated idea of science like Albert Einstein had hypothesized that time is relative, which means on how you perceive it or is it what our faith has told us over the generation of it being pass down. Now, time has started out in man's eyes as far back as when we emerge from the primordial ooze or is it when a spirit of energy has created us. For example: as the sun emerges on the horizon casting an embracing blanket of warmth on life, letting life know that it is time to emerge from its slumber to do its daily activities, and at the end of the day, time is singled when the sun dips down beyond the horizon and the moon emerges, and man has known that this is the time for rest and preparing for the next day. Is time eternal, as it has been pass down in our faith, or does it have a count down?

What if I was to say that they are all true, some of you may know this and others may not. Time is patients, it shows us to grow when it is needed and to rest when it is asked of us. Time is a fickle mistress when we get to know her one minute we are crawling in our diapers the next minute learning to walk and obtaining our precognitive skills. Then we evolved into an obstinate state of mind or life style by lashing out, in a manner of thinking that we know everything and can do everything. One day we wake up, and find ourselves standing in front of the mirror staring at the person that we have become, and wonder. When that moment has arrived to where we see ourselves in the way we began in diapers. We asked ourselves did we have a good life; did I make the right decisions that needed to be made? For all of us, it is a constant internal battle that we struggle with. So, in our final chapter as we lie there, an empty vessel of a husk of the person, a remembrance of who we were, all painted up and put on display for our love ones, is that really the final chapter of our lives? If so, let's pack it in, forget about the future, and the future of our selves in diapers and say screw it. Why bother with rules, being courteous to our fellow man and just push the button and end it all and forget about it. Is there a next chapter? I say yes, if you will indulge me I will explain the reason to this madness as you embark on the journey.

Time has many forms, one can say that time is a straight line that is encumbrance where all things happen in order to show record. While keeping this train of thought on that straight line, a segment of time is a snap shot on the time line that has some significance of record.

Now, time has a peculiar way of stepping out of the normal aspects of thought on occasions. This peculiar thought that you may be so inquisitive about, some people have deemed it to be science fiction, and others believe it is a consortium of religious beliefs. This so-called aberration of thought is known as time travel. Time travel has a universal rule that governs the natural order of things, and one of the rules, if not followed can cause a catastrophic event in the time stream that may have a chaotic hiccup, if you will. For example, let's say that a person or persons had travel back in time, and move an object out of place in the time line, which causes Adolf Hilter to win the war of World War II, and the allies had fallen to the forces of the axis power what would life be like now? This is called the butterfly effect when something like this has occurred.

Another abnormality of the rules of time is known as a paradox. A paradox is an occurrence when you travel to some point in the timeline that is not your own present, and meet the other you, and this causes a ripple effect throughout time. This paradox can alter the timeline and quite possibly alter the fabric of reality itself. For example: it has been widely speculated if you were to merely touch yourself, the you at that timeframe, and the future you will no longer exist ever again, and some say if you just even see yourself it would have the same adverse effect.

Here is the part that a lot of you may not know. The architect that designs the events in the timeline quite possibly be a random of an event, which is also known as the chaotic theory, or maybe it can be the passion of one's religious belief, or quite possibly be both. To whatever extent of the master of the design, when a sequence of events that have happened in that particular time frame is known as an "Epoch". Let me elaborate a little bit on what is an epoch, now time is a straight line from beginning to end, however it's not that simple as you think.

Think of it like this, it's a bow, like on a violin at first you see one massive string, but when you look closer to it there are multiples of strands, like multiple events that are compressed together. An epoch is that such bow on the violin. What all religious and non-religious beliefs can agree upon is this, that at some point in time there will be some kind of an event that will end to all of this. Whether it be some type of scripture or foresight that has to explain the return of their GOD that will destroy those who do not believe and rescue those who do, or some massive implosion which will rain down the destruction of the universe. An epoch is an event that was designed for that specific time frame.

By now you are thinking that this is turning into some type of science fiction novel more than it is a non-fiction book. If you have read this far into the book please indulge me a little more I swear I will get you there. Now, it has been known through the world either by whispers from people in passing, or by simply picking up a book and doing some research on the matter. There are certain religious beliefs that manifest itself as being eternal. For example: Tibetans Buddhist believe in a life cycle. Let me elaborate on this a little, you see the Buddhist believe that we are to be reborn after every death of the flesh, and the only time that we can be at peace is when we find the enlightenment. I will get back to this conversation further down the road, but right now I have to digress on the matter. You see this belief is one variation of an epoch, another form of this epoch is one of the most famous. I'm talking about the book of Revelations in the New Testament, which was written by John the Apostle.

You ask yourself where is he going with this, and what is his intent and motivation of comparing these two religions, I'm not comparing two religions, yet. The epoch is a timeline to where it will happen, however when the actual events that may occur, or may not occur, are they in our life time or in our children's lifetime, who knows for a fact. During these thousands of years, both of these religions have practiced their faith and pass down their beliefs from generation to generation the tradition and values. Both which still stand today, so where is he going with this you ask. The epoch of each is understanding that the end and rebirth of their religion is upon us, and throughout time it has been preached upon to us and yet we still stand. The time frame that this will occur is it this generation or the next one and so on, that is the question of all time are we the generation of this epoch? Are we doom if we don't follow this religion or that one or maybe none at all? Are we to humdrum along with blinders on, and pass our same knowledge and beliefs down to the next generation until we become callous and no longer have compassion and understanding to our fellow human brothermen. Here is my question why can we not see the piece of the puzzle in front of us? Can it be quite possibly that God, or some kind of entity that is vast with infinite wisdom and knowledge has left bits and pieces of the puzzle scatter throughout the world, and time, and throughout all the world religions? If so, is the epoch of end times which we seek so desperately, is it when we collect all those pieces of the puzzle and put them together?

Each religion has their nuance about the beginning and the end. Each of these religions believes so strongly in their faith that it infringes upon the other beliefs creating wars and destruction base on that belief. Take the Jewish and the Muslim faith for instance. Both of them have been creating unspeakable acts to one another over generations that stretch over thousands upon thousands of years. Why is this you ask? What started this hate and turmoil you ask? Was it that one faith trying to control the other, was it the fact that a jealous brother wanted the love and attention of a father that he gave his other son? Was it a misunderstanding between two clans where something went awry? Who knows why, the real reason that truly sparked the war with these two religious beliefs. However, I can tell you that both religions have the same pinnacle father.

Now let's embark on this hypothesis if you will. Throughout time in human history, the cattle wrangler of society was religion, it brought order and consistency to a seasonal year.

With this being said, another two factions go at it, and that would be the World of Science and the World of Religion. One is the belief of creation and the other is the belief of the construct of creation. Can you guess which one is which? If so you may not get it right.

By now you are wondering what in the wild world of sports is this guy talking about. Where is he going with this thought process and what conclusion is he trying to draw. What values or morals is he trying to instill upon in the reader if any at all. In the spirit of good will and the respect to all faiths, this is my journey for you to embark upon. The reader must contain an open mind and be vigilant with respect to patients and understanding. My goal is to draw a unified conclusion of the masses to where God has left pieces of the puzzle not in one faith but all faiths. Yes, you heard it correct this insane lunatic of a person is going to attempt to consolidate the world religions into one big picture that is "The Word of GOD".

You ask yourself what is "The Word of GOD" and what does it mean to you. Could "The Word of GOD" be in all religions, or is it design that one faction will be the result of the chosen one's that everyone's religion talks about, and if so are we playing a crap shoot game with our faith? The answer is yes to all and no to all at the same time. In order for you to understand where I am coming from, I will explain in each of the following chapters "The Word of GOD". By now you may have cast aside the book, or it has found its way in some garbage can in some wretched alley, and quite possibly in the bottom of some waste can in an office building with someone's yogurt drizzle all over it, or whatever the case may be. Well, I implore you not to do so, if you hate it and you are discussed by it, that fact that remains is that you are throwing out insight and knowledge to other religious facts that you may not have known about. What is it worth to you a few minutes of your time that could possibly shed some light on a subject matter that you have been quandary upon for quite some time.

In order for you to understand where I am going with this you have to walk a mile in someone else's shoes, and yes, I know it is a little cliché. When I was born into this world I knew nothing. We are all like this, when we come into this world we are naked and little. We have no idea what to do, how to do it, and what comes next. This is our society today we are infants to the wonders of the universe. The only thing that we know when we come into this world is that we are embrace by love, either by the doctors or nurses of this world, or by our mothers and fathers when we are in their care. We don't know how to feed ourselves, wipe our little tushies, or find something to wear. We embrace the warm milk from our mother's bosom, as well as the firm hand from whoever is changing our diapers, not to mention the attire that we wear. We crawl around on the ground not a care in the world, we know that we will be fed and our diapers change, and again the clothes on our backs will be there. You see the innocence of our lives when we start out is pure. As we look up with that scowl look on our face like we ate something bitter or sour, we know that we went boom

boom in our diapers, and our parents or person of care changes them, we have the same feeling as we look to the stars.

Then we grow, and as we grow we are still innocent to the world. I remember from the stories of my parents how I started to walk. Like most I'm sure is how we all started out is like this. From my own experience, I would race across the floor on all fours and come to a sofa, chair, or some object and slowly pull myself up, kind of like climbing a rock face of a mountain. As my eyes appear over the emerging edge of the surface our legs begin to wobble, seeing how we never have used that muscle, as we suck on that pacifier making gases sounds like we are talking. We look around and admire the scenery, we are swaying back and forth always keeping a firm grasp on the object that we just climb. There in the mist of everything that we are doing, we notice something which seems like miles away, however it is most likely a few paces away. Our target is locked on, and there is no escaping the confines of our only true one thought. That thought is to seek out that object regardless of what it is. My object that I was told, is when my grandfather who had come by for a visit.

Now, I have come from a Keltic background on my mother side of the family which is Scottish and Irish, and my father side is English and German. The object of my grandfather, just so happens to put down his can of beer on the coffee table and walk off to do something. The can of beer was on the other side of the living room. The story goes, my parents had some friends and family over for a visit and people were socializing and noticing me trying to walk as I kept falling down. When my grandfather had put down the can of beer, my mother has always told me that, in that moment I took off like a rocket to that can of beer. I was not grabbing on to any object or having any kind of thought, it just happens. She said one moment I was in eye sight and bam it was off to the races, just like how we are today with our own goals and admirations.

Needless to say, we all have our little quirks and nuances of innocents as we are little.

Once we have motor skills and we start to learn and wonder about the world that we are in. We become rowdy due to the fact that we don't understand what we are doing and our care takers have to discipline us. You see I grew up with two other brothers, and like a good old Keltic family that we were, well we would always try to handle things civil if you know what I mean. At first, I was alone, getting the spot light and nothing to worry about, and then came my brothers Tim, and eleven months later my other brother Jacob. I was four at the time when they had arrived in this world. So, I was already getting into trouble prior to my brothers showing up. My mother and father would always say that I would be playing in the backyard digging and bringing in pockets full of dirt, and whatnots into the house. The look on my mother's face was priceless when she had noticed that what I was bringing in from the outside, from what I was told by my dad. She had a look of disgust, but at the same time a look of horror, like she had seen a ghost. She tells me to empty out my pockets of dirt that I had brought in the house, so like a good boy I did. You thought the look was priceless before, once I remove the fistful of dirt and mud out of my pockets she notices movement in the piles. She asks, what is that over and over with such a high pitch voice. I told her, worms mommy. She had flipped her lid she was in such a state of disarray it was unbelievable. I thought she was going to have a heart attack, however, she took a couple of deep breaths and calmly ask me why did you bring the worms into the home? I reply with this innocent voice of a four-year-old I didn't want the worms to get cold. So, she cleans me up and explains to me that the worms are meant to stay outside because that is where their home is. After she did all that she told me not to do it again as she used to say, "for the love of Pete sake".

Seasons have changed, time has elapsed, into the blink moment of life. We grow older and wiser hopefully. When man had sharpened his skills from a crude rudimentary structure of tools into a more practical instrument of precision. This gives mankind the unlimited bounds to which we can achieve goals of the universe. What does he mean by this you ask? Simple, as I stated before what is mankind striding for and where are we going. When we grow, we develop certain aspects of our motor skills. Our speech becomes more coherent, our action of movement has more precision. We start to understand more on what has been taught to us by our parents, or someone that has been watching over us. We build on this construct of teachings that has been pass down. Whether it is the simple process of doing school work, the fine teachings of someone showing us how to hunt, or our religious leaders. This stage here is the predapiss of the direction that will lead us into the next stage of our life cycle. Not to be crude, however, this is true. Think of it, if you strip away the foundation of race and raise a child just based on beliefs alone of the culture around him or her regardless of their natural background the fundamentals will surely be more prone to their surroundings. For example, do you believe if a certain child's parents were killed and their beliefs where in the ways such as the Muslim faith, and the child has become an orphan and that orphan was raised by a family that was different then the orphan's parent's belief, let say Judaism. Would they let the child suffer an endless turmoil of grief and despair? Do you think that the action of these two worlds colliding that it would be all rainbows and sunshine? Can it be the fundamental of both worlds at first colliding into a downward spiral to which they would find some type of equilibrium, and begin to build a construct of both worlds?

You see when we start learning at some young age of our life that our minds are like a sponge. In which this means that if you are to be violent and teach it to the young ones then they are more acceptable to becoming a violent person, and yes not all will be like that there quite possibly be a certain percentage that might be opposite of that nature. You can say, the flip side of the coin could have the same outcome. Most people can see it as sciences basing it off of human behavior studies, or it could be the Ying and Yang of the nature of things. Most eastern cultures believe in this. Just like science having negative charge particles and positively charge ones the Ying and Yang represents the fundamentals of nature. Out of everything that could go awry, would have some type of enlightenment and out of every enlighten soul, there lurks the darkest of thoughts, to paraphrase.

Depending on our rise to adult hood and the construct that we were brought up can have monumental impact. Now as teenagers, if you will, regardless of our upbringing we break the bounds of our shackles, and venture into the wilderness taking this rebellious mantra. We say and do things that we know deep down is wrong, however, we do them to create our way of life and fulfill our destiny. We, and yes I said we, as the world have been in that state at one point in time. I don't care if you lived in some back-water pole dunk town, some tribal nation in some part of the world, some suburban kid riding his or her skate board, whatever the case maybe we as a nation of homo-sapiens have been there. This means me as well, as a teenager I have pulled some dumb stuff, anything ranging from growing my hair out with black dye trying to look like one of the characters from Ann Rice's book "Interview of the Vampire", to having parties when your parents go away on vacation and take your two younger brothers with them. To having sex in the back seat of the car, and anywhere else you can find a place to do it. Rules at this point in our lives are thrown out the window and we make our own way. There are consequences when we paint outside the box. This can cause us to go down that proverbial downward spiral that lands us into a destruction mode, or we can take a long hard look at our life and fan the flames and pull our self-up like an ace pilot, or a phoenix rising out of the ashes and get back into the fight known as life.

The day has come where we pull back the shrouds of anticipation with that cock strong attitude of that worldly knowledge that you have, and say, "I got this". As you step forward into the world of adult hood there is a pretty good chance that you will fail, if you did not have the proper guidance as a child. With the wrong attitude the instant that you step one foot though that threshold you will fall flat on your face without a doubt. For those of you who are properly prepared, and have listen to a degree, will do decent in the next stage of our lives. For those who belong in the fifty-fifty club like myself there are untold riches. In other words, we could fall or soar. I had two biggest fears at this point in my life, one was that since I came from a lower middle-class income family, that I would be stuck in my shit hole of a town living life like everyone else. I just could not see myself doing this. The other fear that I had since that I came from such a background that I would not be able to see not only other parts of the country, but the world as well. Whatever choice we make as we cross that threshold, I say this be careful of where you step, and at the same time don't be afraid of walking on egg shells. With that said, I weigh and measure my life in a moment of a blink of an eye. I was going nowhere fast, so I decided to go take a test. This test consists of basic fundamentals of what you have learned in your years as a person. I can say I did an outstanding job, which landed me any job that I wanted with this particular corporation. The corporation that I'm talking about is the United States Army. I could of have any job that I wanted, but no I had to choose the front lines. The job that I sign up for was an Infantry soldier man. I thought to myself what better way to see the world and get the hell out of my town. Like most people, we have to find our way, some by a calling to education, or by sports, and others by religious preference, or whatever other way you did, however, this was mine.

When he or she becomes a man or woman there is some type of journey or task that they have to perform. I guess to some of us we can say that we cross that threshold twice. On a religious point of view, we have. Protestants and Catholic faith people the coming of age ceremony is known as confirmation, and in the Judaism, is known as Bar Mitzvah, for the male origins, and for the female is known as Bat Mitzvah, in the Muslim world is it known as Khatam al Quran ceremony. Hinduism would be another famous and oldest religion, which is sometimes that is over looked. Their coming of age ceremony for the males is known as Upanayana for Dvija, and for the young ladies, it is known as Ritushuddhi. These are a few examples of the coming of age ceremonies that may have been, or may not have been overlooked. Each one tells a tail in maturing with their society and religious beliefs. I hope by now that I have given you some insight on some worldly traditions, as well as my own in this chapter.

Chapter 2:

"The Oldest Religion"

Who is the creator of this wonderful life? What is the purpose of whom or what that created the cosmos, and their plan for us and other species to play out? Where did it all begin; was it some type of manifestation of our psyche, or was it the divine intervention from something spectacular? Whether or not if you believe in the beginning as a cosmic eruption of a single singularity creating this ever-expanding universe, creating new life in the pockets of the cosmos, and once it has run its course a huge implosion of some sort. Can creation of everything we see, touch, taste, smell, feel, and experience could it be from something far greater then what we can imagine? However, what we might feel on this matter, we have a beginning as humans, and over the centuries our explanation of how we were created is a wonderment all in itself. Speaking of this wonderment of sorts, where did we get the notion of having beliefs and where did the term "The Gods or God" had emerged from? We needed some type of grounding to establish a type of order in our tribes, villages, towns, cities, or whatever social faction. The world is vast in with many ideas and beliefs of how, who, what, and where we came from.

As many theologians have come to realize how old some religions are, which dates back as far as the fiftieth to eleventh millennium which is fifty thousand B.C.E. to eleven thousand B.C.E. This was just basically when man was living in caves, and just learning how to live in a society. There have been some scholars stating that there is evidence of cave drawings dating back to the Paleolithic era which is approximately four hundred thousand to two hundred thousand B.C.E. In whatever the case may be when the time of man had started isn't the question. The question is as we progress into societies when did religion take a major role in our lives?

It is strange how the development of religion had started with the ideas and the wonderment don't you think. The Beginning of religion, is a lot like how our planet moves. What does he mean by this you ask? Well, as the sun breaks on the eastern horizon slowly passing over us giving this warm glow of embrace to our spirits, and when it finally starts to settle in the west to bring us into a state of slumber, and as the moon emerges. The birth of religion has the same effect to the ways of nature.

Religion was born in the east. Just like the rising of the sun on the horizon from where it has embraced us with the warmth to our spirits. One of the oldest religions that still runs strong today is known as "Sindhu", or also known as "Sanatana Daharma". A lot of you are scratching your heads, how a religion like this that I never heard of still exists today? This religion has over a billion followers, and that derives from the east, not to mention that it still exists today what could he be talking about? Well, it wasn't until later in the fourteenth century when Sindhu had migrated westward to a land known as Persia. The Persians didn't really have what would be a traditional "S" sound in their vocabulary. So, with that being said Sindhu was change to what we know as today is "Hindu".

The birth of Hindu or what a lot of western cultures called today Hinduism is a mystery. You ask how is something that has such a historic timeline still maintain the devotion and the complexity of the traditions over the centuries still be here today? Faith is a powerful montage for a society to believe in. Not all religions have a hero story, or a happy ending let alone an origin story, like a comic book story. By now you are probably asking yourself the wrong question and making the wrong statement. You see the question that you need to be making is this, and keep in mind throughout this book as well. The question you need to be asking is where did the idea come from, and how did it manifest itself into an elegant stream of thought that is still practiced today.

To those who do not believe in this religion show some patience and courtesy as we dive into this world, or some will say peel back the layers like an onion. The beginning of this culture that is known today as "Hinduism" from what I have gather no one is quite sure how it started. Even as I do my research some theologians say that this religion started as early as five thousand to two thousand B.C.E. The majority have stated that it had begun in the "Vedic Era" which is dated to two thousand B.C.E. From this we can have a foot hold or the foundation to begin to understand this culture.

So, we kind of narrow the time frame of the beginning of this belief, but where in the east did it originate from. What providence, country, state, territory did this belief come from you are probably asking or maybe you already know the answer to this question. This story takes place prior to Hinduism. A group of people that were known as the "Aryavarta" which later became to be known as "Aryans". Their civilization originated from the Scythians region of the world. Which many historians and scholars of sorts have also named them Indo-European culture. The Scythians culture had laid dominion north of the Black Sea, engulfing the areas around the Caspian Sea, and also encompassing other regions, to what are now known as today as: Kazakhstan, Uzbekistan, Afghanistan, Kyrgyzstan, Turkmenistan, Pakistan, Parts of Georgia and Azerbaijan, and far west as the Ukraine.

So, the stage is set, we have the time frame, and the region of the manifestation of this belief. The Aryans were a primitive society, who spoke a language that was known as Sanskrit. They were not a very bright society, when it came to things with other societies, in other words, the bulk of the civilization was illiterate. They were a war-mongering nation, that was involved in gambling, drinking, womanizing, however, they did have a sense of elegant storytelling, especially when it came to their gods. One of those stories is about their God known as Dyaus Pitar (sky god).

The story goes something like this, In the beginning, was nothing, no heavens, no earth, and not even the emptiness in-between. The story continues when the spirit said, "let me be warm" and he created fire to keep himself warm at night, and as an indirect way from fire, the light was created from this. Does this sound familiar to anyone? Let's continue on shall we.

It wasn't until the Vedic era that the Aryan people invaded the northwestern region of what is now known as India. When they invaded the region of Indus Valley they had control of the people and started to enthrall the people of this region with their culture and ideas. These beliefs later had matriculated down through India.

Now Dyaus Pitar is the father of Gods at this time. It is said that when he created man that he was given the gift of everlasting life. Other gods fear man, because they felt that man would become like gods themselves, and they wanted Dyaus to do something about this. So, he did, he created woman, and which brought sexual desires and wanting more to distract man from achieving the goal's to be like a God. Then the world became over populated, and from this Dyaus has seen that man was immortal why would they need gods. Keeping his promise to the other gods he had decided to make man mortal. Which was the birth of the Goddess of Death, and from her tears she brought death to mankind. She didn't rule over the dominion of death, she was the embodiment of death itself. Now keep in mind this is still the Aryan's beliefs that are being passed down.

It wasn't until later in the Vedic era, that the Indian nation had fought back to win their freedom, however, they still had sub-stain the Aryan's beliefs of the God's. Today the Hindu faith rejects this idea, due to the fact, of how the western nineteen-century scholars had portrayed solely based on what they had found in their research, however in their scriptures they do refer to the Aryan's, and their beliefs. To this date scholars debate over whether or not who is right on this matter.

In the Hindu faith, just like other faiths, there are teachers, and priests if you will, and they are known as Pujari or Archaka. Pujari are split in the middle of this notion, however, some of the Aryan's beliefs have survived over the millennium in their scriptures which are known as the Vedas. Veda translated loosely to english means wisdom. Vedas is their Bible, their Torah, their Quran, it is their sacred text that they hold holy. It is consisting of four books or Vedas which are Rigveda, the Yajurveda, the Samaveda and the Atharvaveda, and each one of these Veda has subtext or books and they are known as the Samhitas, the Aranyakas, the Brahmanas, and the Upanishads.

In any case, whom ever is right on the matter, over time the Indian people started to embrace the ways of the Aryan's beliefs, and as the stories have been written and rewritten, and have been told over camp fires over and over, from generation to generation. The Indian people over time have laid claim to their ways by changing the god's names, and by adding some more of their own. What was known as Dyaus Pitar is now known as Brahma. Brahma has many faces to him, but he is the creator of all. When other gods and goddess were formed, they were created from him. Brahma created other gods and goddess such as Vishnu the preserver; who's purpose was to maintain order and harmony of the universe. Then there was Shiva the destroyer; his intent as a god to bring destruction to the universe so it can be recreated. Ganapati the remover of obstacles, Saraswati the goddess of learning, Parvati the goddess of love, and many others to follow. The Hindu faith have many gods and goddess, demigods and goddess as well as avatars; however, we only have time to hit the highlights of this faith.

The Hindu faith is a wonderful tapestry of vibrant colors, and wonderful depictions of man and animal. The great detail of their faith and the devotion that has lasted over the centuries is truly remarkable. One of my favorite stories about this culture, is about a little boy, and how he came to be. His birth is like a Greek tragedy; however, it happens to have a happy twist to it; sort of speak.

The god of destruction, which is Shiva, his task was to destroy the universe in order for it to be rebuilt. Now, Shiva, was always admired by his followers, and he tried to please them as best as he could. One of his followers was one not like the rest, who has worship him, he was a demon king, known as Gajasura. Gajasura has always given great penance to Shiva. Once Shiva had heard the prayers of Gajasura, he asked Shiva for a boon for himself. Gajasura graciously asks Shiva, to enter his stomach, not only allowing him to be closer to Shiva, it would also allow him to draw from Shiva strength. Shiva was vain in these matters to his worshipers, so he granted Gajasura his request.

Shiva had a wife, she was the Goddess of fertility and love, and her name was Parvati.

Her story goes, while she was drawing her bath, and there was no one around to guard the house. Meanwhile, Shiva was trapped in the belly of Gajasura the demon king, which has a peculiar look to him, he has a head of an elephant. After spending time in his belly, he was wanting to get back to his wife, who at the time, is about to take a bath.

Since there was no one around to guard the house, and before she emerges herself into the hot soapy water, she bent down and grab a handful of earth and started to mold it into a vessel of a little boy. While Parvati was molding the vessel of the little boy. Trying to return home to his wife, Shiva freed himself with the help from the other gods, in which he had landed Gajasura's body, without a head. His wife, at the time had no one to watch over her, so she breathes life into the vessel of the boy that she had just molded from the earth, and told him under no circumstances that she was to be disturbed. Shiva has returned to his betrothed and notices this boy. As he tries to pass the boy, not knowing who he was, wasn't going to let him pass. Shiva made haste to the boy, and Parvati notices the boy's demise and she started to weep. Now there are several variations of this story. The end result is this; Brahma, had helped by breathing life back into the boy, however the boy head was no longer useable, so Shiva had to replace it, and he did, with the demon king's head. The boy's name which is known today as Ganesha.

It is truly an amazing culture, and the depth and love of their faith is truly a wonderment. There are many Gods and Goddess, not to mention demi gods and goddess as well as demons. I ask you this, some of the anecdotes that their faith may or may not sound familiar to you, and if not that's quite understandable. Who can argue the fact that Hinduism is the oldest religion and not to mention over a billion followers worldwide? My question is this, is this the religion that we follow, or is this the stepping stone of the piece of the puzzle that lies ahead of us? Only time will tell as you read on.

Chapter 3:

"The Expansion Of The East"

Since this explosion of gods and goddess by the Hindu faith, and enough time has elapsed into the ether. There was a great awaking of hope and prosperity for the future of mankind, however with the rise of this new hope also the rise of hate and violence. When there is good, there will be evil, and when there is evil, there will be hope. For what I'm about to tell you, there are three different, but unified in one thought, and that is peace. Some will say that they are a religion, and others would say no, because it's more than a religion it's a way of life. What I'm about to embark on, are the teachings that sprung up from a war-torn nation that has plagued the innocents by corrupt emperors, and tyrants that were so hell bent on power. Hope needed help to grow in ways that people thirst water in the desert.

Now, this is roughly about fifteen hundred years later, give or take a couple of hundreds of years, that these new religions, or way of life which ever one you wish to prefer had sprung up in the east. The three unifications of thought that I'm about to talk about, all happen roughly around the same time of each other. The three are what are known today as Buddhism, Taoism, and Confucianism. Each in their right have brought a way of thinking for the betterment of mankind and expanding on the glimmer of light of hope.

In my research, I have discovered no exact pin point on where each one had started. I can tell you that they all roughly happen around the six hundred B.C.E. Each one had no easy task to carry the torch of hope to their beliefs. I would love to start in order of things, however, since there is no real-time frame of each one I would like to start with ways of Buddha.

Buddha was a real person and not a god. He was what you can call in some eyes a prophet bringing the teachings of hope and peace. Buddha Shakyamuni, was born with a silver spoon in his mouth. He was a prince from a wealthy family that lived in the northern province of India. He was destined for great things for his family. He had servants that catered to his every whim. He went to the finest schools, and was tutored by the greatest minds of the time. The boy was well versed in the ways of the Hindu faith. Everything that a prince life that you ever wanted, it was picture perfect.

You ask yourself, if he had it so great why or how did he become the father of what is today the fourth largest religion in the world. Well, his father was a proud and noble man, and he felt highly of his son's innocents and wanted to protect him from the outside world. So, through his youth Siddhartha live a glorious but shelter life. He did not know what hunger, sick, or the way of a poor person had to live, and not to mention the struggles they had to endure. His life was set, and with not a care in the world what so ever. He even had a prearrange wedding to a beautiful woman by the name of Rahula. They said at the time of his birth that Siddhartha was either going to be a great ruler of the people of his nation, or a wise spiritual leader. So, at this point in time, he was surrounded by love and beauty, not knowing the flip side of the coin. Until one day he had asked his father if he can visit the local town.

The moment you asked how he achieved such greatness in this era, well it was a journey to the town some may say, and others may say his first steps to enlightenment was after he had visited the towns people. His father worries about his son's innocence, so he orders all the sick, lame, and old to be removed from the town as he passes through. However, Siddhartha did happen to come across an old sickly man that was sitting in an alley. He wonders what happen to him, how did he become this way. Why was he so skinny and why is his skin so wrinkly and why are his teeth so mangled and why was his hair white, as he is asking these questions to himself. In a total shock and dismay, he thought to himself he had to return to the town and see more. When he returned to his father and explain what he saw on his journey, his father had forbidden him to ever return to the town. However, he had made two other trips back into town without his father's knowledge, in order to see the town's underbelly of society, if you will.

At the age of twenty-nine, he embarks on a journey for knowledge and enlightenment. Siddhartha had made a decision to leave his wife and child behind without thought, to go on and explore the lands of his father's kingdom, and meeting the people of these lands which had different back grounds and obtaining the knowledge of life. Some may say he was a dead-beat father for doing this, however, if you live your whole life in one realm without knowing what is outside and you had the opportunity, or wisdom, or wealth maybe you might have done the same thing.

His journey was like most, they were filled with trials and tribulation. Now, most of you think Buddha was this pot belly man of an Asian descent, that was famous for something spiritual. Well, the truth of it all, he wasn't always like that. On his journey to enlightenment, he was a beggar of food and shelter. He notices the wisdom through his starvation, and that is when he discovered that he needed to fill his belly with food, both physically and spiritually. It has been said that he sat under a tree for a day, however some say that day lasted a longer duration of time, and this is where he came to Nirvana. From this, his teachings are known far and wide, they are known as the Four Nobel Truths and the Eight-Fold Path. Through this, he teaches people how to become one with the universe through the mind set of observation, meditation, and honest living. Is Buddha a false prophet, or a prophet of God that was yet to be discovered? Is this faith wrong for believing in a way of honest living with a spiritual mind set towards being one with the universe? Is this religion another stepping stone, on how God wanted us to understand the ways of enlightenment? Only time will tell.

The next enclave from the east, is a man by the name of Kong Qiu which he also created a way of thinking just like Buddha. His teachings also expanded on how people should treat each other through wisdom and understanding. His story, takes place in China during the Zhou dynasty which is about one thousand forty-six or five to roughly two hundred and twenty-one B.C.E. This is a long span of time, however, there are two settings to the natural order of things in this belief. By now you are asking which culture of religion is he talking about. Like all things, there are beginnings and ends to everything.

Kong Qiu was born in the province of Zou which is near Qufu, China. The names of the region and time frame were mainly ones that had deep meaning to them. Kong is a name of the particular clan of his family, Qiu is the name, or given name that refers to the gender, however, there are many translations of this name, but what people know him by today is Confucius.

Now, Confucius's father had died when he was three years old, and he was raised by his mother, not like Buddha who came from wealth, he was raised in a world of destitute. His life struggles started early, while living under the local lords known as Lu. Coming from this back ground he knew he wanted more in life, and this provided him with the willingness to achieve his goals. Since he has grown up into an impoverished state, at such a young age, he grew up with the understanding of what hardship is, with the values and morals of human kind. So, when he started a family at the age of nineteen with a woman by the name of Qiguan he understood the gravity what it takes to be a family man.

It wasn't until he was in his early twenties that he had sustain jobs in the local government. He worked as a bookkeeper, horse wrangler, and as a shepherd. He maintained his education in the schools at the time to better himself and provide for his family. It wasn't until the loss of his mother at the age of twenty-three when it had hit him hard, he mourns his mother's death for three years. With the tragic loss of his mother and his growing family, he moved forward with determination. As he progressed in life as a young man he advanced in status, and eventually becoming a teacher by the age of thirty. He was a teacher of six arts, some say that this was his first steps into the ways of enlightenment. He taught calligraphy, ritual, charioteering, music, and archery, he also had a deep fondness for history and poetry that help to develop his teachings skills.

It wasn't until his late forties that he stepped into politics where he became governor of a local town. His official title was Minister of public affairs, which was a minor position in the course of things. He quickly moved to the Minister of Crime where his next struggles had accumulated. The region was ruled by a Duke at the time in the Lu province, and within this area lived three of the most powerful families. Now, he wanted to centralize the government, however, you see each of the families had these walls, and Confucius wanted them to be taken down. The neighboring faction known as Qi notice this and thought that Lu province would have become a powerful nation, and so Qi had set upon its demise. As Confucius set out in trying to take these walls down to make way for a centralized government he made powerful enemies in the region. He had started to make great strides towards his goals, however, in doing so he failed to gain support and in return, he resigned his position.

In his exile state, he journeys to the northern province areas where he teaches and becomes a student of life. From this state, he also came to his version of Nirvana through his teachings. Now, there is no book like the for-mention religions, however, he did have scripts and poetry. His teachings like Buddha were merely the teachings of honor and good living. He tried to instill upon the practice of good family, where you honor your father and mother, not to mention your neighbor. He also believes in being a God-fearing man. So, Confucianism is the way and understanding of life and how to treat others in the process. Is this truly the way to believe, or should we ignore this way? Is Confucianism another stone on the path to Gods Word? Let's journey on shall we.

The final, but not the least member from the east is one that is surrounded by great mystery. The mastery of the art of motion and mixed in the ideas of the way of the universe, some can say that the legendary art of Kung Fu had started from this religion. I remember when me and my brothers try to master the arts of Kung Fu from watching all the old movies, just like I'm sure some of you did. This particular way of thought is also a philosophy just like Buddhism, and Confucianism, however not like the for-mention dogma it is a religion that was decreed in the Tang Dynasty. This religion was started by a man by the name of Lao-Tzu around the same time that Confucius started. Both have very similar ways of thought, however, Lao-Tzu believed that the way of Tao or Taoism also known as Daoism is the embracing the way of the path. You ask what does Lao-Tzu mean by this. Confucius embrace the way of order and harmony to whereas Tao embraces the ways of chaos. If you ask if Tao is chaos then how come so many followers believe in this way, and is chaos a force of evil? In the way of Tao is embracing everything and through everything, there is no order which it follows, so in this case, chaos is knowledge.

Just like the Hindu faith which believes that all gods are directly manifestation of Brahma, Taoism also believes that all ways lead back to Tao. The reason is this, we all are different in a lot of ways and no one can do the exact same thing. Let me explain; regardless how two similar entities are the same there is something that separates them, and this is what is known as the path. Lao-Tzu did not come this way by any easy means, he also struggled through life like Buddha and Confucius. His story is one that comes in mystery, the reason that you ask this, is because there are three men that have the similar names and came from the same region of China. The only thing that I can gather on him about his early life that is factual is this, he was born around six hundred and one B.C.E., and during the Zhou Dynasty, he establishes himself as an historian in the royal courts. There have been speculations of his pass, but no one seems to know a whole lot about him. One legend says that he spent eight or maybe eighty years in his mother's womb, things like this. The only thing that all the scholars can agree upon is his legacy of Tao.

Lao-Tzu legacy that everyone can agree upon is this, after spending time as the royal historian he got fed up with all the corruption and wanted to retire from society. The story that I'm about to tell you is one for the eons. The journey of Lao-Tzu was like all the others, middle age as we see today, however, it was late in life during this time era. On his way out of China, and away from all the corruption of society he embarks on his Nirvana when he came to a gate keeper to the land beyond China. The man asked Lao if he had anything to declare before moving on, and he replies, "I only have my knowledge that I have gained in my life" (I'm paraphrasing this), which was known as Tao, which loosely translated into English as the "Way" or "Path". So before leaving, he sat down using the wisdom and knowledge of what he gained over time on this plain of existence, to write a book some will say others a collection of poems which is known by Tao Te Ching or Daodjing. Tao teachings are simply what all mankind stride towards, and that is simply love, compassion, kindness, moderation, simplicity, frugality, humility, and modesty. From this one can find the major fundamentals to enlightenment, and unlocking the way of the universe, once he had finished the writings he turns his work over to the gate keeper and vanishes into the west. Is the journey that we seek, is it in the journey itself? Is Tao the one we should look towards as our path? Is this another stone that God wants us to put on the path of enlightenment? Let's let the candle burn shall we.

I know that I have not immersed you into the fathoms of each of these religions, however, I just needed to highlight some areas to spark your attention. Some will say I have not truly done any of these ways justice, and others will say what is the point that he is trying to make in all of this. I can assure you that if you have the patience and time I will explain all of this. I wish that I could have immersed you further into the each one of these teachings, and if I did this book would turn out to be as thick as Webster's Dictionary.

Chapter 4:

"The Movement Westward"

As religion spreads across the ancient world like wild fire, it moves west, back into the regions from where it all started from, the land from which the Aryan's had come from. For what I'm about to talk about will cover a little more in-depth than the previous ones, not because of favoritism, but of the complexity of it all, and how young they are compare to the for-mention practices. The three religions that will expand over the next three chapters are known today as Judaism, Islam, and Catholicism. These three religions are the major main beliefs of today, and highly volatile in the worlds eye. Since these religious beliefs are so strong and highly controversial I ask to please hear the facts before making an outcry of one accord or another.

I will start with the oldest member of these three in this chapter. I will begin with the faith of Judaism, which comes from the Hebrew nation and what are known as Jews today. Now before we just dive right in the religion we are going to go back to where it all started from to get a better grasp of the big picture of things.

The story begins in an outlet, where the Atlantic Ocean has carved an open channel where three continents have surrounded this particular body of water. As this body of water pushes eastward, where the waves break on the shores of the Canaan civilization. The Canaan civilization region is what is known as today as Syria, Israel, Lebanon, and the southern portion of Turkey. The Canaanites culture dates back as early as the fifteen century B.C.E. which is about fifteen-hundred B.C.E. Since the region of the Canaan people where located off the shores of what is known as today the Mediterranean Sea, the area was prime for agriculture and had great value to trade routes. The Canaan people spoke a language which is known by Semtic, which the language dates back even further then the Canaan people. The Canaan people had their versions of Gods and Goddess, and the primary God and Goddess were called Baalim & Baalot.

Now, the Canaan people, had the nation of Mesopotamia to the east to trade and contend with, and not to mention they had the Egyptian empire to the southwest. There was another contender that the Canaan people had to deal with, and they were known as Mitanni and they were base in the north. Mitanni are a part of the culture that I had previously stated known as the Indo-Europeans which the Aryan culture was a part of. During this era, everything was based on either horse back or camels for trade and migration of society. With the increasing pressure from all sides eventually, something was bound to have happened.

With all these cultures and ideology of beliefs, there was bound to have some overlay in stories, and since there was no internet, or other modern technology to fact check everything, the belief system was based on whoever or whatever faction was in power, and the camp fire stories that were told from one clan to another, one generation to another. The three mention empires started to encroach into the region of Canaan, and bringing their way of life and their stories, and one famous story does stick out and that is known as the flood. There are two variations of this story, and both versions are separated by time and cultures of beliefs, however, they could be one in the same. One is well-known by the name of Noah, however, there is another man, known by the name of Utnapishtim.

I would like to start with Utnapishtim, the reason for this is that this story comes from the east out of the Mesopotamia culture that dates prior to the famous story of Noah that some may say. There was a king by the name of Gilgamesh who ruled over Uruk located near the Tigris and the Euphrates River which would be considered today as Iraq. From King Gilgamesh is where our story of the flood truly begins, he was truly a brilliant ruler of this time. He had achieved what no other king in this region could ever possibly accomplish, however like all things there is an end. Gilgamesh did not want to go down without a fight. The man sought out the adventure of a lifetime, he wanted to become timeless, immortal. In his adventures in trying to find immortality, he stumbles upon a man by the name of Utnapishtim. He explains to Gilgamesh, that he was task to build a great boat by the God's, in which he went into great detail that he had to bring all creatures onto this boat by pairs and also his family and friends. Gilgamesh returns to Uruk with stories of his great exploits of his adventures, however not ever finding the cure for immortality that he was seeking, but he did live on through ancient text and stories.

The Judaism faith comes from the ancient texts, scrolls, or books, in whatever manner of your choice to call it, but it is known to them as the Tanakh. The Tanakh makes up of twenty- four books to what some people view as the old testament. In the Torah, the first five books are known as Bereshit (Genesis), Shemot (Exodus), Vayikra (Leviticus), Bamidbar (Numbers), and D' varim (Deuteronomy), these are important, because a man by the name of Moses had written them. The Nevi'im (Prophets) makes up the second set of books which are known as Yehôshúa' (Joshua), Shophtim (Judges), Shmû'ēl (Samuel), M'lakhim (Kings), Yesha'ăyāhû (Isaiah), Yirmyāhû (Jeremiah), and Yekhezqiēl (Ezekiel). Some people are thinking now wait a minute I know that is not the true order of old testament which in fact it is true if you were talking about the old testament. Then you have what is known as the Twelve Minor Prophets which basically is one book that is consist of twelve chapters. They are: Hôshēa'(Hosea), Yô'ēl (Joel), 'Āmôs (Amos), 'Ōvadhyāh (Obadiah), Yônāh (Jonah), Mîkhāh (Micah), Nakhûm (Nahum), Khăvhakûk (Habakkuk), Tsephanyāh (Zephaniah), Khaggai (Haggai), Zkharyāh (Zechariah), and Mal'ākhî (Malachi).

The remaining eleven books are known as the Ketuvim which are poetic readings that are mention in the seasonal times of the Judaism faith. They are: Tehillim (Psalms), Mishlei (Book of Proverbs), and Iyyôbh (Book of Job) are what are known as the three poetic books (Sifrei Emet). The next set of books are mention only during certain religious holidays like the following five books: Shīr Hashīrīm (Song of Songs) or (Song of Solomon) which is mainly read in the time of

Passover (is the celebratory time when Judaism people left Egypt by their leader Moses), Rūth (Book of Ruth) the time of Shavuot which is (a major festival held on the 6th, and sometimes the 7th sabbath fifty days after the second day of Passover which was originally a harvest festival). Eikhah (Lamentations) the season of Tisha B'Av also known as Kinnot (is the time of the Judaism faith comes together and mourns the loss of the first and second temple in Jerusalem, as well as other great atrocities that have happened to their faith). Qōheleth (Ecclesiastes) the season of Sukkot (this is known as the Feast of Tabernacles or also known as the Feast of the Ingathering). Estēr (Book of Esther) this is the season of Purim (commemorates the saving of the Judaism people from King Haman who wanted to kill the faith in one fell swoop). The last three books are: Dānî'ēl (Book of Daniel), 'Ezrā (Book of Ezra or also known as the Book of Nehemiah), and Divrei ha-Yamim (Chronicles)

In the book of Bereshit which is the first book of the Torah, it depicts of how creation had begun. Just like the for-mention beliefs, there is a beginning from where it all started from. In the scriptures of Bereshit the first book in chapter one verse one through thirty-one and chapter two verse one through two it says:

["*In the beginning of God's creation of the heavens and the earth. Now the earth was astonishingly empty, and darkness was on the face of the deep, and the spirit of God was hovering over the face of the water. And God said, "Let there be light," and there was light. And God saw the light that it was good, and God separated between the light and between the darkness. And God called the light day, and the darkness He called night, and it was evening and it was morning, one day. And God said, "Let there be an expanse in the midst of the water, and let it be a separation between water and water." And God made the expanse and it separated between the water that was below the expanse and the water that was above the expanse, and it was so. And God called the expanse Heaven, and it was evening, and it was morning, a second day. And God said, "Let the water that is beneath the heavens gather into one place, and let the dry land appear," and it was so. And God called the dry land earth, and the gathering of the waters He called seas, and God saw that it was good. And God said, "Let the earth sprout vegetation, seed yielding herbs and fruit trees producing fruit according to its kind in which its seed is found, on the earth," and it was so. And the earth gave forth vegetation, seed yielding herbs according to its kind, and trees producing fruit, in which its seed is found, according to its kind, and God saw that it was good. And it was evening, and it was morning, a third day. And God said, "Let there be luminaries in the expanse of the heavens, to separate between the day and between the night, and they shall be for signs and for appointed seasons and for days and years. And they shall be for luminaries in the expanse of the heavens to shed light upon the earth." And it was so. And God made the two great luminaries: the great luminary to rule the day and the lesser luminary to rule the night, and the stars. And God placed them in the expanse of the heavens to shed light upon the earth. And to rule over the day and over the night, and to separate between the light and between the darkness, and God saw that it was good. And it was evening, and it was morning, a fourth day. And God said, "Let the waters swarm a swarming of living creatures, and let fowl fly over the earth, across the expanse of the heavens." And God created the great sea monsters, and every living creature that crawls, with which the waters swarmed, according to their kind, and every winged fowl, according to its kind, and God saw that it was good. And God blessed them, saying, "Be fruitful and multiply, and fill the waters of the seas, and let the fowl multiply upon the earth." And it was evening, and it was morning, a fifth day. And God said, "Let the earth bring forth living creatures according to their kind, cattle and creeping things and the beasts of the earth according to their kind," and it was so. And God made the beasts of the earth according to their kind and the cattle according to their kind, and all the creeping things of the ground according to their kind, and God saw that it was good. And God said, "Let us make man in our image, after our likeness, and they shall rule over the fish of the sea and over the fowl of the heaven and over the animals and over all the earth and over all the creeping things that creep upon the earth." And God created man in His image; in the image of God He created him; male and female He created them. And God blessed them, and God said to them, "Be fruitful and multiply and fill the earth and subdue it, and rule over the fish of the sea and over the fowl of the sky and over all the beasts that tread upon the earth. " And God said, "Behold, I have given you every seed-bearing herb, which is upon the surface of the entire earth, and every tree that has seed bearing fruit; it will be yours for food. And to all the beasts of the earth and to all the fowl of the heavens, and to everything that moves upon the earth, in which there is a living spirit, every green herb to eat," and it was so. And God saw all that He had made, and behold it was very good, and it was evening and it was morning, the sixth day. Now the heavens and the earth were completed and all their host. And God completed on the seventh day His work that He did, and He abstained on the seventh day from all His work that He did. And God blessed the seventh day and He hallowed it, for thereon He abstained from all His work that God created to do".]*

So, we have the story of creation, but you have not told us when or where did Judaism had started, or let alone the story of the flood. The Torah is the first five books, and was written by a man named Moses who we will get to on a later note. He illustrates about the beginning of creation, The Tower of Babble, the story of the Great Flood, and many other stories. Now since creation has been taken into account, and the growing society of Adam and Eve is spreading across the land, people are having such ways with each other that would be considered unholy, and even by today standards.

You are probably asking who is Adam and Eve, and some of you already know. To sum it up Adam and Eve according to the Bereshit (Genesis), they were the first man and woman that was created by God. They had three sons, however, the first two sons were famous, for the story of the first murder in history, and the third son according to the text was a mere mention. Since the death of Able by his brother Cain, God had cast him out, and banish him into the desert, not to be heard from again. This is the start of the story that caused the Great Flood. It was mention that Adam and Eve had a third son by the name of Seth. Now Cain, in the wilderness by himself, came upon his new wife that will provide him with his sons, and her name is unknown at this time. The population of the Cain tribe grew, and with the evilness lurking in the shadows awaiting to rear its ugly head again. The second murder along with other sins that have accrued through the great nation of Cain, God had enough with this sinful taste of mankind, so he called out to a man by the name of Noah, and instructs him to build a boat for every two of the same creature and his family. The flood came to wash out the sinners of that time leaving Noah and his family on the boat without land in sight for forty days and nights. After the flood waters have receded back into the earth the population of the earth swell once again with a fresh start.

So, the new family tree, of all the people today, are now trace back to Noah's family which is traced back to Adam and Eve. Now, why do we all speak a different language and have different ways of going about things, if we come from one family? That would be the story of the Tower of Babel. This is a synopsis of the story of the tower, a King by the name of Nimrod in the land that was called Shinar (Assyria/Mesopotamia region). The King was trying to construct a building that would reach the God's and in doing so one day it all came to an end and the people that once spoke the same language mere hours before the collapse of the tower now cannot understand their neighbor or relative. Thus, is the reason why we all speak different and from that, we have different ways of thinking as a culture.

You can say the father is Noah and the mother is Naamah in the biological since however, there is another father one of the spiritual faith that sets just underneath God. Not only that he is the father of Judaism, he was also the father of the Islamic faith and Catholicism. You ask who is this person, well he goes by the name of Abraham. Abraham grew up in a city what was known as Ur. This city was located on the banks of the Euphrates River just before opening up into the what is known today as the Persian Gulf, and happen to be the capital of the Mesopotamia Empire at the time, which was a few miles away from the city of Uruk give or take a hundred miles.

Sometime has passed and his family left the city of Ur and headed northwest along the Euphrates River trade route to a town called Haran. This city was located in what is known as today the country of Syria, and there he met his wife Sarai and he was devoted to her. He lived in the city to the age of seventy-five years old, and this is when he got the call from his God. It has been prophesized that he headed southwest into the land of Canaan. This was not a land that he was familiar to him except only through whispers. So, he took his wife and his nephew by the name of Lot, and his people to this land that was filled with war-mongering nomads. He rested in the towns of Shechem and Beth-el and thus the true journey of the three nations had begun.

There was a great famine that spread across the nation of Canaan, so Abraham move once more. This time into the nation of the Egyptian Empire. According to some scholars, they say that his God did not tell him to go into the land of Egypt. So, Abraham with the thought of the survival of his family and followers moved into the land of Egypt. The story goes something like this, in fear of losing his life and his wife Sarai, who at the time was deemed a gorgeous woman, he would introduce her to the Pharaoh of Egypt as his sister. The plan backfired and the Pharaoh had decided to take Sarai as one of his many wives. The God of Abraham got angry and curse the Pharaoh with a sickness of some accord. The Pharaoh later found out the truth behind what was going on and banish Abraham back where he had come from with his wife and the carts of wealth that was given to him by the Pharaoh. The Pharaoh's name is not known according to the scriptures.

So, back into the land of Canaan, he goes with his wealth narrowly escaping with his life and his wife and the members of the tribe. At this time of his life with his lovely wife has not father any children and they have tried according to some scholars. Whether it was the age of Abraham being as old as he was or maybe the fact that his wife could not conceive a child. It looks bad for the both of them, in the eyes of everyone in the tribe that was following him.

During this time, a woman would be considered to be worthless if she could not conceive a child, and a man that could not, especially in a position of leadership, was deemed as unfit and was looked upon with great shame and disrespect. They knew what they were facing, with their local society. Sarai went to her husband with great humility and said to lay with a servant woman. Abraham outrage with this notion that his wife had concocted, was loyal to his wife and said no, however after moments of her pleading with him for the sake of saving face in front of the whole tribe he agreed to the terms that his wife Sarai had set before him.

In the scriptures, it was said that Abraham's God had told him that he will have a son with Sarai, however, in saving face in front of the community he had lay with the young servant girl by the name of Hagar who nine months later gave birth to a child by the name of Ishmael. Sarai seeing the fault was not with her husband, but with her, she grew worried that Abraham will grow tired of her. She had grown into a state of depression and anxiety as she watches over time the relationship that her husband had with his bastard son Ishmael. Ishmael has grown into a fine young lad unaware of the politics that surrounded him. Sarai falling into a black hole of despair heard a voice from the God of Abraham saying she will conceive a child. Abraham hearing of this news had neglected Hagar, who grew jealous of what is about to come. That she would lose all of her status that she had just gained. As she went from a servant girl giving birth to the leader of the tribe one and only son, to once again joining the ranks of the lower class.

As Sarai started to show, nine months later she gave birthto a son by the name of Isaac.

When Sarai had given birth, she would be considered a great great grandmother in today's world, and not to mention that it would be as much as five times over by their standards. The reason is, she gave birth at the age of eighty some years old. Now labor is tough on a woman in her prime, however giving birth at that age is double or maybe triple the pain. Two sons, two mothers and one father, however one was born out of marriage and the other was born from an old woman. The reason I'm telling you is because, Abraham was the father of the three nations of Judaism which is Isaac and his other son Ishmael is the birth of Islam. You said three nations but you only mention two, the third nation was born from the bosom of the Judaism faith which we will go into more in depth later. So, Abraham was told by his God that he will be the father of many nations, as many as the stars in the heavens.

As Isaac becomes a young man, the two women grew more and more impatient with each other, and Abraham had to make a decision. He asked Hagar and her son Ismael to leave the tribe and set out before that there was more conflict that will arise in their circle. I know you can imagine the discontent that Hagar had with Sarai after hearing of this news by Abraham, and seeing that she had to leave the tribe and set out on her own with Ismael I'm sure that her anger grew even more, however that story does not end there.

The religious faith of Judaism begins with the journey of Isaac the son of Abraham and Sarai. The recent departure of Hagar and her son Ismael had left a void in Abraham's heart, never the less Isaac had some shoes to fill in accordance to his father, and the practices of his father's God. Like some flowers that blossom in a short time when the weather is right, the family of Abraham was also a mirror image of the same resounding resemblance to the for- mention flower.

Now that the mother giving birth at a very old age even by today's standards, and the father of the same accord, was now asked by God to create a great atrocity in the eyes of Abraham. The God of Abraham directed him to take his son Isaac to the top of Moriah and sacrifice him in his name. Abraham thought that his God was joking in jest and had asked his God why and are you sure, and his God replies with a serious resounding voice to sacrifice his only son that he waited for a long time to have by his only wife, which had given birth to, in her golden years.

Today the Judaism faith recognizes this event as the Akedah or Aqedah which is also known as the binding of Isaac. Now, Isaac was not a mere child when Abraham's God called him to do this task, Isaac was about thirty some years old. So, at this time when Abraham was fighting himself at every corner giving himself every reason not to do this, is finding himself tying his son to a stone altar. Most of you are saying, since he is a thirty something-year-old man what could be possibly be going through his mind at this time, and most of you are saying I would have done this or that to make my way out of this dire strait. You have to understand the time frame that they are in as well as the faith of the community to their God.

The stage is set his only son tied down on this stone altar, and the timeless Abraham raising a dagger just above his son that his God had promised him, and Sarai at that moment getting an eerie feeling, like that of a title wave just about to hit a canoe. With all of his aging might in one swift blow he plunges the dagger into Isaac, however just mere centimeters away from his abdomen Abraham's God with an acoustic sound that would put one hundred fog horns put together to shame, had said stop. Abraham, at that moment like any other father in the world looking at what he was about to do, drop the dagger and then dropped to his knees in tears. Abraham weeping with thousands of emotions going through him, and cried out why, why God, and his God reply I wanted to test your faith. As his God, just had said to him stop, a ram had appeared from behind a bush, and that was to be a sacrifice in the place of Isaac. In the Judaism faith, this is also known as Rosh Hashanah which it signifies by blowing into a ram's horn.

Just like that, a whole religious faith could have been snuff out like a candle in a drafty old castle. Alas, Isaac's trials and tribulations were not over yet. The return from Moriah with the sacrificed ram that took Isaac's place on the altar, Sarai rushing over to her baby and embracing him like she would not see him again. Now there are two versions of this story just like anything some scholars say it was a torch and others say it was a dagger, just as well it was an object of destruction that was about to take a life. The same goes for the return back from Moriah some say Isaac did not return and others say he did, however, the end result was Sarai was old and weak, and that eerie feeling that she had, finally did her in. It was said that she was buried in a cave, called Machpelah, also known as the cave of the Patriarchs, where this is the resting place of Adam and Eve as well as Abraham himself.

Sometime has passed, and Isaac was now forty years old, and it was time for him to take a wife. He chooses a lady, which his father has chosen for him by the name of Rebeckah which happens to be his second cousin. Her grandfather was Abraham's brother, by the name of Nohar. They had two sons by the name of Jacob and Esau which later would take the knowledge of their father's and grandfather's faith, and stories and pass it down for generations to come. Jacob married two women, and had relations with two other women by the name of Rachel, Leah, Zilpah, Bilhah, and between all of them he had thirteen children.

With his first wife Rachel, he had Joseph and Benjamin. His second wife Leah he had Reuben, Simeon, Levi, Judah, Issachar, Zebulun, and his only daughter Dinah. With the two handmaidens Bilhah who gave birth to Dan and Naphtali and the other handmaiden Zilpah who gave birth to Gad and Asher. The twelve tribes of the Judaism faith are called: Reuben, Simeon, Levi, Judah, Dan, Naphtali, Gad, Asher, Issachar, Zebulun, Joseph, and Benjamin. These twelve started out where their great grandfather Abraham had nearly escape with his life, and his family's life from the land of Egypt. Since the tribes of Judaism had found their way back into the land of Egypt, this is where I leave you with the story of Moses. Is the Judaism faith truly the chosen ones? Is this the faith that we have to fall in line in order to be the chosen ones? Could this be another chapter in the Word of God?

Chapter 5:

"The Banish One"

Since we last heard of Hagar and her son Ismael, they were banished into the wilderness by Abraham by way of Sarai to avoid any conflict that might have occured. They have been roaming aimlessly through the desert, on the brink of dying of thirst with hardly any water in their rations to sustain the both of them, Hagar in fear of her world coming to an end and seeing her son die right next to her had to make a decision. With the supplies running low and in fear of losing her son, she was truly a loving mother to the last ounce of her life, she was about to do the most heroic act, she was going to commit suicide. Once again, right before the act was about to occur, just like that, what had happened with Abraham and Isaac when God said stop, God had shown her a well to nourish her and Ismael back to life. Since there were no grocery stores and drive-thru's, and they needed to eat, so Ismael had to learn how to hunt and in doing so became an expert archer.

As they were making their way out of the wilderness of Paran they had found themselves in the land of Egypt. The same land that his father was told by his God not to go, and almost losing his, and his family life. Now, after surviving the long and arduous journey they need to find a place to settle and make their way in the world. Hagar knew she was getting old and needed her son to live and pass on the legacy, so she had to find a good woman for her son, and she did, with a simple common woman to marry her son off.

Sometime had passed, and the passing of his mother hit him hard, and the news of her death was widely whispered, which eventually had gotten back to his father. Abraham had set out on a journey back into the land of Egypt, however this time he had come alone, to pay his respects and to see his son's new wife. While Ismael was out providing for his family, his father had stopped by to see Ismael and his wife. He had appeared to her as an old but distinguished of a man, and had asked her a couple of inquisitive questions about how are things and how she perceives her living conditions. When Ishmael had returned, she had mentioned that an old man had stopped by, and had asked her some questions, Ismael reply "what did he have to say", so she told him about the questions and that he had a message for him, he asked "what was the message" and she replies, "that you are to change the gate to your home". You see Abraham ask the young lady two main questions one being how is life and the other was are you doing well to sustain the home? With those questions, he asked of her and her replies were "poor and that we are struggling to get by and we live in a poor home". When Ishmael had heard what his father had asked of her and his message to him, he knew that she was not the right woman for him. Ishmael had remarried and again Abraham had revisited the young woman, however she had a different tone than the last woman that he married, and Abraham was pleased with this one.

The reason of the two stories is that the young woman of Egyptian origin is unknown, and not to mention how many wives that he took, and as well their names. Ishmael had twelve sons, and their names are: Nebaioth, Kedar, Adbeel, Mibsam, Mishma, Dumah, Massa, Hadar, Tema, Jetur, Naphish, and Kedema, and just like the twelve tribes of Judaism, these were the twelve tribes of Ishmael which later grew into the twelve tribes of Islam. Ishmael also had two daughters as well, by the names of Mahalath and Basemath.

Ishmael's brother Isaac had two sons Jacob and Esau, we know the story of Jacob already, however, the story of Isaac's other son was not told. Esau was a simple man that indulge himself with the ways of the arts. He was the eldest of the two brothers and he took more of a backseat role when it came to Jacob. Never the less he was a man and he was looking for a good woman. Just like any man of this era, Esau was no different in the matters of taking wives, and one of those wives so happen to be his uncle's daughter, Mahalath. Separated by two different mothers the house of Isaac and the house of Ishmael once again had re-emerged with each other.

The question still remains, so where did Islam begin, and why did Ishmael have an epiphany that skewered from his father's faith? Did his father's God tell him to practice in a different way, or was it the enticing beliefs that surrounded him in the region of Egypt? The answer is no and yes, you see Ishmael did hold firm to the faith of his father, but through his son Kedar, the faith of Islam had begun. What do you mean by this you ask, well his son Kedar made his way back to the land of his grandfather, back from where it all started from, back into the land of Mesopotamia, on the shores where the Tigris and the Euphrates had come together on the banks of what is known today as the Persian Gulf/Arabian Gulf. The Kingdom of Qedar (Kedar) was a vast empire of nomads that travel the country side that traded with one settlement to another. Through the region of desolate wastelands where natural resources were scarce, and communication between societies was few and far between. Where an ocean of time, and the spread of Kedar people had swell. They had become what was known then and still known as today, the Arab nation or world, and this stretch across the lands that are we know today as Saudi Arabia, Yemen, Qatar, United Arab of Emirates, and Oman.

This is where the story of the Islamic faith had taken place. We come to an area where a boy born into this world around five hundred and seventy years A.D. As an orphan that was raised by his uncle Abu Talib went by the name of Muhammad Abdullah. He was born in the city of Makkah (Mecca) which would be located near the Red Sea in the country what is known today as Saudi Arabia. By his birth, the nomadic empire had spread throughout this region and later became known as the Arabia. The Mesopotamia also went by another name which was known as the Persian Empire, that still stood fast in the east, and to the north, the old Canaan nation was no longer in the west and the Egyptian Empire had fallen to the same adversary which was known as the Roman Empire. There was a smaller nation to the north, beyond the horizon of the Roman and Persian Empires, and they were known as the Armenia Empire.

Living in this region, a lot of time has passed between the nation of Kedar and not to mention the distance from where Kedar had started in the land of Mesopotamia. There has been some, but not all people who had stay true the ways of Abraham. The young man grew up in middle of all this corruption and paganistic beliefs of this God or that God. He grew up to be a fine merchant in the city of Makkah. By the age of twenty-five he was married to a woman Khadijah, however, he had a total of eleven wives when it was all said and done, but Khadijah was his true love. Everything seems to be going good with the young man a good job that he excels at, an obedient wife and wives, and the people seem to like him not only as a business man but as a friend as well.

So, what gave him the idea or thought to lead a new nation of ideas and religion that was so different from his forefathers? He had become tired with the level of pollutants in the society that had surrounded him and his family, so he had decided to leave because he felt that he needed a change. Since his recent departure from the city, he needed time to contemplate on how to change the wickedness of the society that surrounded him and his family. However, some can say that he was prophesized to become a great person. The reason why is that there was a story prior to him having this epiphany that made him leave the city, and it goes something like this, Muhammed while traveling outside the realm of the city, was unaware what was going on, there happen to be a fire that just burnt down a holy building. This particular building was holding a precious gem that was said to date back to Adam and Eve era. During the construction of a new building, no one tribe could come to an agreement to whom would be the one to set the precious gem back into the building. So, they came to the conclusion that the very next person that had come across their path was the one to set it back into the building.

When the ceremony of the stone was to be placed back into the building the leaders of the four clans had held a corner of a shroud, and with the help of Muhammed who was the one that was chosen to place the black gem onto the shroud as the four clan leaders carried it to the spot where Muhammed would place the gem into the building. Today that so-called building is known as the Kaaba which is best describes as a square structure that sets in the city of Makkah which houses the black precious gem, and is compared to the Judaism Tabernacle, the Holy of Holies place of worship.

During his time of meditation, it was said when he left the town to a nearby cave where he settled for quite some time. At the age of forty is when he received the word of God. An angel came down from the heavens by the name of Archangel Gabriel, which gave him a command to read the scriptures that he had presented to him, however, Muhammed could not read or write, and he told Gabriel this. Gabriel again commanded him to read the scriptures that he had presented to him, before he was about to squeezed the life out of him he replies I cannot, so, when Gabriel had released him, he started to read the scriptures to him. As he was listening to the sound of Gabriel's voice, which he was so astonished by his voice, it gave him such clarity that he remembers every detail of every word that he spoke. Knowing this he had to share it with his people, The Word of God. Just like his forefathers prior to him he was once again spreading the word of the God of Abraham. From what he was told by the angel, he also regaled that he was the last prophet to spread the word of Allah the one true God, the Judaism faith call him Yahweh. Separated by tongues and time the message of the God of Abraham was to continue through the eyes of a young man, and former merchant, is to be known as the Prophet Muhammed.

Just like all things new when starting out he did not have many followers at first, and he was driven out of Makkah along with his followers. They set out into the wilderness, and had come to a city by the name of Yathrib (Medina) that was to the north of Makkah by a few hundred miles. This journey marks the beginning of the Islamic calendar which is known as Hijrah which took place in the year six hundred twenty-two A.D. His numbers swell during this time, the reason was he had brought peace to the local tribes that have been fighting with each other and with the tribes around Makkah. In the midst of his followers swelling to the tenths of thousands he manages to regain Makkah, however, he didn't take his revenge out on those that exile him from the city, instead, he had forgiven them and change the rules of the town.

Just like the Judaism faith and the other religions that have been mention, there is a holy book, and the Islamic holy book is known as the

Quran. Since the teachings of the Prophet Muhammad had started to the day of his death, he had unified the nations of the Arab world, and from his death, the Quran was born. The Quran is the message from God by the way of the Archangel Gabriel to the lips of Muhammad Abdullah, and like any book, it has an author to take the word from a higher power, and to put it into scripture. The Quran itself is consist of one hundred and fourteen Surahs (chapters) and several hundred Ayat (verses).

Since the birth of the Islamic faith through the Prophet Muhammad there are several celebrations that take place, and they are: Muharram (The Islamic New Year; beginning of the Islamic liturgical year from when Muhammad emigrated from Mecca to Medina on July sixteen, six hundred and twenty-two A.D.), Mawlid al-Nabi (Prophet Muhammad's Birthday), Eid al-Fitr (The Celebration concluding Ramadan the month of fasting), Eid al-Adha (The celebration concluding the Hajj, or the Feast of Sacrifice, commemorates the prophet Abraham's willingness to obey Allah by sacrificing his son Isaac). From the book, itself and its celebrations that are similar to the Judaism faith. The main embodiment mainly practices the way on how to be better people, by teaching them how to get along with one another, without judgment or hate from one faction or another, just like how some of the eastern philosophy or religion are depicted. Is the Prophet Muhammad the last one or was there another that was the last one? Is the belief of the ways of Islam the correct path to take? Could this be another stone on the path to the Word of God?

Chapter 6:

"The Prodigal Son"

The Canaan nation has been riddled with one faction or another, and when this so- called faction would take over this region they would lay waste to the Canaan civilization, and making it suitable for their own ways. Since the ensuing encounter of Abraham's and his two sons, there has been another takeover of this region, and its thirst for power had rival its predecessors in the ways of battle tactician, modern weaponry, and the endless supply of greed and empty promises of power to those who would help topple their enemies. This unstoppable war machine was the Roman Empire, and their leader was fear and was revered by many, he went by the name of Julius Caesar, and his name would be Rome's title as Emperor. Julius Caesar is responsible for laying waste to lands as far north to what is known as the United Kingdom, most of the European countries, and moving east through the nations of Greece, and driving his force into the Arab nations, which already has been plagued with wars of conquering nations, and holy incursions amongst the tribes of this region over the years.

Julius is not only known for his ways of trying to conquer the world, he also had a philosophical nature to him. He was responsible for what is known as today as the Julian Calendar, which gives us the days and months of the year. You ever wonder why we measure time in B.C. or B.C.E. to A.D and what it all means? According to scholars prior to the Julian calendar was the Roman Empire calendar which was known as the Commonwealth calendar, and it was based off the moon phases, which a committee was put together, that determine the adding and removing of days. In his conquest of not only controlling the world, he needed to control destiny, in his way he had found himself in the city of Alexandrian in search of someone that could help him with this dilemma. With the help of certain mathematician, astronomer, and practice in the ways like his mentor Socrates was a man by the name of Sosigenes. A century prior to Galileo Galilei he based his findings off the revolution of the planet around the sun which he took the idea from the Egyptian solar calendar.

Julius Caesar reign of power as Caesar the dictator was only for ten years in doing so he had accomplished more than most men could. Not only he took ideas and made it his, for everyone to follow in a state of order, like what he did with the calendar, he also took the ideas of God's from other cultures and made it Roman's. He took the Greek God's and incorporated into Roman's way like Zeus for example, the father of all God's is known as Jupiter, and the God of the sea Poseidon was renamed as Neptune, and so on. With his demise in forty-four B.C.E., where he was betrayed by the senate of the Roman Empire in a gathering of debate, another man came forward to rule as the new Caesar his name was Augustus Tiberius.

Since Julius Caesar went from a general leading the armies of the Roman Republic to leading them as Roman's Caesar as a dictator implementing his ideas and ways throughout the region of his conquering lands. Some ideas took longer than most to have manifested, like his idea of time keeping. Even though he needed a fundamental way of keeping time to bring order to disorder, he himself was caught up in the era of B.C.E. and his successor usher in the transformation of his legacy. You see B.C or B.C.E. and A.D. are three terms that have a religious aspect tied to it. B.C. (stands for before Christ, which we will get to later), B.C.E. is a new term which was introduced centuries later (stands for before correct error), and A.D. is how we measure time today and its relationship is (Anno Domini, is Latin, for in the year of our Lord).

Now there is no year zero if you ever wonder it went simply from the year one B.C. or B.C.E. to the year one A.D.

A man by the name of Tiberius Claudius Nero also known as Augustus Tiberius was the Roman Emperor at the time when this particular son was born. His reign of power started around twenty-seven B.C.E. to fourteen A.D. He was the nephew of the great Julius Caesar, he was well known for taking back Rome by force, from the corrupt Senate that killed his uncle, and not to mention his arch enemy Mark Anthony. You see Mark Anthony was Julius right-hand man, and he made accusations towards Augustus saying that the only way he was the rightful heir was that he had relations with Julius.

Now, as you can see Rome was in turmoil with this all going on, and a certain son was about to be born into this world. Most scholars and historians can't agree on the exact time when this child was born, however, they can estimate to be between three B.C.E. and one A.D. The season or part of the year that they also can narrow it down to, would be around June or July. In any case the story of Jesus Christ in accordance with the Holy Bible or The Holy Scripture, his story is spread across several books. The book of Matthew, Mark, Luke, and John, which these are also known as the Holy Gospel in the faith of Catholicism which we will get to later. Since the birth of light, and since the birth of man into existence, there was no other birth that could rival the birth of this particular son known as Jesus Christ.

When Abraham had his two sons, Isaac and Ishmael the lineage of Abraham once again plays an important role. When Sarai gave birth to Isaac which in turn gave birth to the Judaism faith, another birth gave birth to faith as well. The birth of Jesus Christ was the predapiss to which the birth of Catholicism had begun. While Rome was in turmoil, another ruler was about to reveal himself during this time. He was vain of a man, he was self-indulging, and his ego was as high as the clouds and he wanted to be the center of attention in everyone's eyes. His ego demanded that everyone had to bow and worship him like no other, and his particular name was King Herod. Now, he had heard of the prophecy that was about to come to fruition, one that would take his spot light away and he couldn't have allowed this to happen.

Jesus was born to his mother; however, she was like no other woman in history giving birth to a child. What do you mean by this, well she was giving birth as a virgin she had not lay with another man what so ever. His father is what you will call now a day's an adopted father, and he is known as Joseph and he was a part of the Abraham lineage through Isaac thrice times fourteen generations, in other words, three sets of fourteen generation of this lineage. His mother was proclaimed to Joseph; however, fate had intervened in a matter where only faith is the strong hold. An angel by the name of Archangel Gabriel had appeared to her according to Luke 1:30, and said "Do not be afraid, Mary; you have found favor with God. You will conceived and give birth to a son, and you are to call him Jesus".

In the timeframe that they were living in would be consider a fear full one, the reason is this, when people don't understand they get scared and emotional, and it gets the better of them. This is what happens to uneducated people, with that being said Mary was showing, and the people were calling her names like harlot, devil woman, and many other names, because Joseph and Mary were not married yet. Right before the towns, people were going to stone her to death is when Joseph stepped in and claimed the child as his. With the shame that was hanging over their head and the news of King Herod in search of the child that would take his glory, they had decided to leave the town of Nazareth and headed towards the town of Bethlehem.

The distance was long, and Mary had sat upon a donkey the entire trip as Joseph walk beside her the whole way, exhausted from the arduous journey they needed a place to rest. At the time Bethlehem had no vacancies, however, they did come to an inn where Joseph pleaded with the Inn keeper for a room and that they would take anything to rest. The Inn keeper had granted them access to the stables out back.

When Mary and Joseph were settling in for the night Joseph knew that she was on the verge of giving birth to her son, he had to make preparations for the child. As Joseph was doing so, another story was on the horizon one that speaks of three wise men from the Arab nation which where called the Magi. These three men and their followers had come to see the birth of this prophecy, and in doing so they had brought certain gifts that each one gave. Their journey was also long and not knowing which way to go to find this miracle a star had led them the way. When Mary finally had given birth to the prodigal son, all who needed to be there were there to see this miracle.

You ask, how can a religion is just born from merely a child, like all things there is the beginning, middle, and end. Now, the Son of

God also known as Jesus of Nazarene which later be known as Jesus Christ, is in his thirties. As a young man, and prior to him becoming the man that was known as the Messiah, he was also a carpenter. He traveled to a town where a man by the name of John was anointing people in God's name by plunging them into the river and blessing them. John which later was known as John the Baptist, had baptized Jesus in the same way as everyone else, however, according to Matthew 3:13-17 it states: "As soon as Jesus was baptized, he went up out of the water. At that moment heaven was opened, and he saw the Spirit of God descending like a dove and alighting on him". From this point of time, Jesus would be known as the Messiah for the people, and he went from town to town teaching the word of God and doing miracles. As time went on he grew older as well did his fame, and a certain element took notice from this, an old foe had re-emerged, King Herod. This time the Judaism faith also had notice, you see their religious leaders were known as Pharisees, and it was long that the Messiah that they believe would come in like a lion and not a son that was born in the stables. They became worried that a man was going around and calling himself the Messiah.

Since he was doing miracles to the people of the nation like curing the blind, the sick, people with leprosy, and other acts of good work. They felt that he would cause chaos and discontent in their religious belief.

As Jesus was going around teaching the word of God and doing random acts of miracles he was creating enemies, and his greatest enemy was a powerful one that was known to man by many names. This element tried to sway the way of Jesus while he was in the desert by showing him the future and what he could have if he would worship him instead of God.

Knowing his fate, he was reluctant to budge from his ways, and he commands that certain element to be gone and it was gone.

Since Jesus did not marry or had any relations with a woman, ergo he did not have children, however, he did have twelve tribes just like Judaism, and the Islamic faith, and they were known as his twelve apostles. Some can say in a lot of ways they were his children. During the celebrations of Passover Jesus had arrived at this town called Jerusalem, which by entering this town on the back of a mule, like a king returning from a glorious battle, and with his twelve apostles and other followers, following by his side. This is known as Palm Sunday in the belief of Catholicism. Jesus knew that this was the last leg of his journey so he had dinner with the twelve, this would later become the infamous last supper, and at this supper, he gave a prayer which is also known today as communion in the Catholicism faith.

When Jesus was done praying during this last supper, He said that one of you will betray me, and he was right, he went by the name of Judas. Now, Judas turns Jesus into the local Pharisees for thirty pieces of silver. The Roman ruler over these lands was not Caesar himself, but a ruler of the Roman Empire never the less, he went by the name of Pontius Pilate. You see the Pharisees could not condemn a person to death without the official rule of Rome. Pontius did not want anything to do with this nuisance that the Pharisees had brought to his attention. To a means to an end, Pontius and the Pharisees agree to leave it up to the people to decide his fate. The people had chosen a violent killer and thief known as Barabbas to be let go instead of Jesus, the son of David, the son of Abraham, the son of God. So, by order of Pontius Pilate through the people demands, Jesus was to be crucified, and for good measure the Romans had mocked him, whip him, and sat a crown of thorns upon his head.

The Pharisees believed they were doing right by getting rid of a person that was creating dissension amongst their people. The Romans did not care one way or another, and his mother, the twelve and his followers wept as he was nailed to the cross. When he passed, a Roman soldier drove a spear into the side of Jesus to ensure his death, before releasing him to his loved ones. As they prepared his body for burial wrapping him in gauze and laying him in a tomb where it needed a hand full of men to push this giant boulder in front of the tomb to seal it. When his mother, the twelve disciples and some followers had morn his loss for few days, and when a follower by the name of Mary Magdalene came to pray for Jesus at his tomb on the third day she notices that stone was removed and his body was gone. The news had spread fast to everyone, the twelve knew that he had risen, however this had sent a shock wave not only to the Pharisees but to the Roman leader Pontius Pilot as well. At first everyone thought it was a prank, or someone had stolen the body, however, to those who did believe knew that he has risen from the dead, but to those who did not believe, could not fathom his resurrection from the dead.

According to John 20:19 "On the evening of that first, day of the week, when the disciples were together, with the doors locked for fear of the Jewish leaders, Jesus came and stood among them and said, "Peace be with you!".

Through the teachings of Jesus and now through teachings of the twelve a new religion had come to fruition. Now, today Catholicism is a hodgepodge of beliefs following the practice of Jesus and the Holy Bible. On one side, you have the Catholic faith which entails Roman Catholic, Catholic, and what is known as the Russian Orthodox Catholic. On the other side, you have the Protestant faith which is made up of the following Lutheran (Martin Luther Father of the Protestant movement), Baptist, Southern Baptist, Methodist, Southern Methodist, Episcopalian, Apostolic Reformation and many others like the Lutheran belief which is to follow the Holy Scriptures, and not implement their beliefs on how they see the Bible to be.

Catholicism Bible shares the same practice as the Judaism faith. How do you ask, well the Holy Bible is consisting of sixty-six books, one set is known as the Old Testament and the other set is known as the New Testament. The Old Testament is based off the Judaism version of the Bible which is known to them as the Tanakh. The New Testament is consisting of twenty- seven books which includes the famous book of Revelation, that is the foreshadowing to our demise. The Judaism faith does not recognize the New Testament and Jesus as the Messiah still to this day, and they are still awaiting for the day that an entity will manifest itself. I ask you is Catholicism or to some known as Christianity is the way or path that God has instructed for us to follow? Are we to believe that this guy was the third trinity of the Father? Where these stories accurate and did these miracles that were witness to hundreds really real? There is only one way to find out.

Chapter 7:

"The Unholy"

How do you know what is right and what is wrong? Sure, you can say base on your background that this is bad and that, or maybe base off your religion is another possibly. Can you pick out the monster under your bed or in your closet, or what about, how and where you live your life? Ask yourself what is bad or evil, if you have a problem with asking yourself that then ask yourself what is good and holy? What is the decipher between the two, and can one live without the other? Now a day's you have this faction or that faction calling that they are holy and the others are unholy, and vice a versa. So much that both parties are willing to die for their cause and destroy the other party, and the party that is calling to be holy sometimes that faction itself has some people that are calling it to be unholy. So, I ask this what is unholy?

There are many other religious beliefs that have not been spoken about throughout time, because it was deemed unholy. One is known as Devil Worshipping the God of the underworld. This deity went by many names, in the ancient Egypt known as Anubis or Osiris, in Greek and Roman beliefs they are known as Hades/Pluto, Ares/Mars, some called him Beelzebub, Satan, Lucifer, the fallen one the list goes on. In every corner of the world, there is a name for the unholy the one who brings fear and death into the world and goes bump in the night.

It has been said, that some cultures preach that there was a great war between this fallen one and God. Some can say that God created the unholy prior to it becoming unholy. Some can say that they are intertwined with each other and can't escape the perils of each other grasps. The most famous story of this deity is that it was an angel that God created and seeing that angels have no soul this deity became outraged with jealousy when God created man in his image. This deity was cast down to the underworld and brings a plague to mankind whom it loathes.

Throughout time there have been many practices in the demonic realm of conjuring up the spirits of the dead. One is known as Witchcraft, some can argue that there is good in Witchcraft like being a witch of nature and beauty. Mainly Witchcraft is known for its demonic reasons of all sorts. Voodoo is a form of Witchcraft that can bind souls to together with a doll and again other demonic ways. In essence, the Demonic Realm is where your nightmares are born and keep you in fear of. What you have deemed as something that makes you be afraid, will create harm to yourself or others, and that can have ill will thoughts, is known to be unholy.

With this being said, they say that the greatest trick that the Devil has ever done was to make you think that he was never there. I have said before, that even those who have claimed to be holy are in fact unholy I will be given several examples from a variety backgrounds to give you a better idea of things.

Have you ever wonder where the true story of Bloody Mary, and where it truly came from? I can say that she was a demon or an enchantress of some accord, however, she was not any of those, she was a God-fearing woman. The story takes place in sixteen century England where she was born to King Henry the VIII who was also famous for beheading his wives. She grew up with a strong constitutional background in religion which so happens to be the Catholic faith. Now, a man going by the name of Martin Luther was a young monk that was excommunicated from the Catholic faith base on his apocryphal ninety-five writings according to the Catholic Church. Which stated that the Catholic Church was in the wrong for their ways of translating the Holy Bible to the people through teachings and other practices.

Bloody Mary, also known as Mary the first or Mary Tudor, at the time was just starting out in life. Martin in fear of his life left Rome and headed to a land which is now called Germany. As Marry grew in the Catholic faith taking after her father's traits, and him being who he was, had grown into a very cunning woman of sorts. Martin started a religious movement then that is still popular today known as the Protestant Faith. When Mary had become ruler of Ireland and England during the late fifteen-hundreds, she was steadfast in the Catholic faith and saw that Protestantism was the work of the devil, and that any one that believes in that manner was to be hanged, quartered, and beheaded in the town square where everyone could see their heretic ways. Who is to say she was wrong for believing in the ways of her faith, or who is to say that the ways of her faith at the time failed the people? Was the Papacy tainted by the actions of Pope Alexander VI? Did the Devil work in the Catholic faith at the time because of Pope Clement VII? Was the Devil working with Martin Luther? Did the entity inspire Mary to do those atrocities in the name of God?

The Pilgrims went to the land of the America's in search of new prosperity, and freedom of religion. This story takes place on the banks of the Massachusetts shores, in a town known as Salem. The education level of the general public would be considered elementary level compare to today, and without the fundamentals of knowing something that they can hold, touch, or even understand in their way, there will always be something that is bound to happen. The Salem Witch Trials are a blithe on human society everywhere not to mention on America history, though the good people of the town wanted to do good, they had failed in their own teachings of their faith. In some cases, there may have been proof of some demonic acts that were causing harm to the people of the town, however the majority of it where false accusations and innocent people that were put to death. Did the people truly felt that evil was in the town, or did they failed to understand things, and was their faith tested? Did the Devil once again use the ways to tear down the walls of God?

Another incident had happened prior to the Salem Witch Trials, about two-hundred years prior. In the name of the Lord, I cast you out from here, leave this poor merciful person alone Satan, as they would say things like this in a gloomy dungeon somewhere where rules don't apply to them in the name of God. Their blood trails and screams, as people being tortured alive, heads rolling across the ground like a dung beetle rolling its food. What religion is this you ask? Well, the Catholic faith in the early fifteen-century in a country known as Spain, which later would be called the Spanish Inquisition Trials. They would have committed great atrocities in the name of the faith in matters which they deemed to be heretic towards the faith. There was one man that sticks out, his name is Giordano Bruno. He was a man of the cloth just like Martin Luther, and he pointed out some ways of the church were wrong.

Giordano was also a philosopher, mathematician, poet, and star gazer that he had ideas about the universe. He too, like so many prior to him and after him, have said that the universe as they knew about was too small and that the sun did not revolve around the earth, it was the other way around. In the year of fifteen ninety-three after roaming all of Europe teaching people of his theories, had found himself tied to a stake in a town square after being found guilty by the Spanish Inquisition. He was burnt at the stake, in front of everyone, was it due to the level of education, was it dealt in the manner that the devil would spread his lies, or did faith of the Catholic church failed once again to protect their people?

Now, the Muslim Faith base on the Quran, is actually based on the premise of peace and prosperity, as Mohammed had attended it to be by the will of God. Now a day's a lot of fear is being spread throughout the world in the name of this Holy religion. Do you think that the devil is using this faction to implement the demonic ways or once again did the faith failed to guide its followers into the path of peace and prosperity as God had attended to be?

Judaism faith is a struggle that has been as old as time some might say. Coming from the same father in the body and spiritually like its two other religious brothers. The plague of the faith that has been riddled in time. For example: when Moses had delivered them out of bondage from Egypt they were told to follow the ways of God. Not more than a week goes by, they had built a golden false idol that they used for a celebration. The man that came down from the mountain with the rules of God etched in stone and not to mention that he delivered them from Egypt by the will of God turn right around and mock God. Was this the trick of the one who proclaims that he was never there or yet again did the faith failed their followers?

Religious faith, is it all an act to have control of the world or is the hope and peace that we all seem to strive for in our lives? If all religion does is cast people aside that don't believe in their way, but these people are fundamentally pure in the ways of honest living and regardless of their thought, the color of their skin, or a simple upbringing, are these people evil? The big three I like to take a moment to talk about. If they are all wanting to find the path to God, but in the process, they had lay destruction in their path. There was a time that all three had come together in the Arab world and they were all looking for the way to God, Yahweh, and Allah, this was known as the Holy Crusades. At this time, did fear get to these people, did the devil trap the minds of men, where these religious factions righteous in their ways, did God give up on them or was this his plan to make them see that they belong together?

You see not only the boogeyman or some gnarly gruesome demon spinning out of control in someone, is evil. Throughout time people have wanting to do good so bad and so domineering that they lose sight of what they were trying to accomplish in that way they too become evil. Evil takes on many forms in any kind of situation, it can be up front like devil worshipping, can be some demon escaping the clutches of hell by way of summing it or other means. Evil, can come to you in a form of a handshake, leadership, or within yourself. Will evil ever go away? The answer is no, however, there is hope in containing what you don't want to be free. Be careful when you go knocking on certain doors, what you seek may be waiting for you.

Chapter 8:

"The Miscellaneous Ones"

You ever put a puzzle together, or had some type of erector set, and you had something that you wonder why it was a part of the project, that you can do without? In the big picture of things those little nuances that may not be necessary to you at that moment, however when you take a step back and look at it, and you say to yourself that needs something. It might be that a certain fabric that is woven in the tapestry, that little doodad that you wonder why it was there, to begin with, or some type of adhesive binding the project together. So, in this chapter, I will be just hitting the highlights of certain miscellaneous religion, in hopes of you understanding the concept.

What is Religion? Well the definition of religion is a person or group that is set in a system of the same beliefs and practices, is one aspect, and another aspect is a person or group that worships a deity of some accord with the same belief practices. The reason that I bring this up is this there are two factions that I know of, and both of these factions simply just don't believe in the latter of the two definitions. One is known as Atheist and the other is Agnostic, the two have very similar backgrounds. Whether or not they want to admit it or not, they are also a religious aspect in the world. Atheist are people that have a lack of faith or in complete disbelief of some type of deity in the world. An Agnostic person or persons believe in nothing can be known or gain about religion or a deity of any kind. This is quite a conundrum that these two are, in choosing not believing in a faction they become a faction. Why are you bringing this up, you are probably asking? The flip side of the coin did you ever take the time to wonder why they are in such a disbelief of religion?

To gain some insight of this background I have to come clean to you. I was one of these two factions, yes at one point in my life I did choose to turn my back on faith. You see some people do because of an event or events that happen in one's life. The fuel of outrage and disconnection one has in choosing not to believe is not hard what so ever. As I stated in the previous chapter, some people see that religion is the manifestation on how to control society in their thoughts and ideas and not allowing growth or ingenuity of one thoughts and ideas.

Whatever the case may be, is it true that the Church, or people in faith like to call it Mount Zion, have they gone too far in the past to atone for their actions? Is the Church responsible for that disconnection in faith? People, that choose not to believe are they tired of being ostracized by the world? Do they do it for attention or do they have a legitimate concern with the world of faith? This does not mean that these people are devil worshipers or the fact that they hate society, most people who live this life style are good honest people that care, however, they just want to be left alone, and not have to worry about this faith of this faction or that one, in order to get along with people in the world. Like me, most people, but not all did come from faith as they were growing up. In spite of everything there is hope that one day they might find something that suits them to come back to believing again, or they might not, and if you are truly a person of faith then you know you can't judge regardless how you feel about that person's aspect, that is not for you to decide. If you truly do not believe in faith or in some deity, I do wish you well and you do have that right, at the same time if you do decide to come back into the faith do it for you and not for the church, and I hope you can find that relationship with you and your God.

Have you ever been scammed, had something stolen from you, or that you wanted something and you have stolen it and you made up some kind of lie to cover it up. A person of faith would never do that; you say, and if they have, they have asked for forgiveness and atone for it. This religious entanglement makes you scratch your head, however never the less it is a growing religious belief. It took place in the early eighteen-hundreds in upstate New York. A man by the name of Joseph Smith, and the religion that he had started and still going strong is known as the Mormon Faith, or Church of Latter Day Saints. Their belief system still believes in the Holy Bible; however, it has a peculiar twist to it. Joseph Smith had medical issues growing up and his family also did not partake in the religious aspect of things.

His family had to move due to failed business ventures and mishaps, and it so happen that they had landed in a town that was highly religious that was going through a celebration at the time known as the Second Great Awaking. Now, people at the time had a lot of faith, and once again the education level during these times for an average person was very subpar. The story goes like this, Smith had said an angel directed him to buried a book written on golden plates containing the religious history of an ancient people, and he experienced a series of visions, and he needed help to spread the word, however, did not have a whole lot of money to do so.

A man by the name of Brigham Young, who was a wealthy industrialist of sorts at the time. After hearing what Joseph had to say about his visions, he had decided to help him out, with the start of this adventure. Some people can say that Joseph con Young out of money, and others say that Young con people to expand his empire, who knows. Is this a true religion? Do people have the right to believe in a system that makes them feel good? Was the ancient people that Joseph was talking about, were they the Aryans? Did a man con a man or did a man con a nation of believers? Is faith in the Holy Scriptures still presides in this belief? Did the church once again fail its people to allow this belief to occur as a direct result of disconnection from the church, or is the relationship with God destroy in this way of believing?

For what I'm about to tell you in these next couple of paragraphs you do need to keep an open mind. As man had evolved in the ways of spiritually, emotionally, physically, and educationally we maintain one common constant relationship in all. That the fact in every aspect of evolution, there has been trials and tribulation. Since it is about evolution, this is why I'm bringing this up, and not Darwinism (not yet), but in religion and science. There is a difference between science and science fiction, however, both have open doors into each other's worlds. What do you mean by this you ask? The T.V. show Star Trek and the movie Star Wars both had inspired young minds to create new and wonderful ideas that we have today. Another aspect is SYFY books that have also had the same adverse effect on the thought process on how the universe might work, and how we came into existence. Which brings me to my next point the world of SYFY and the world of Religion is a new outlook on life some might say. This new way of thinking on a whole new plane of existence is known as Scientology.

You ask, what part of history, or what Bible, Torah, Quran, or any other holy text did this come from? Well, a man by the name of L. Ron Hubbard was a simple man, a man of science and ideas about the astral plane, and the concept that we came from another world and the path back to that world is through the evolution of the mind and knowledge of science. This had spark a lot of people in the nineteen-fifties to start thinking like this and movement is still strong today as it was then. The reason for this belief as Mr. Hubbard has put it "A civilization without insanity, without criminals and without war; where the world can prosper and honest beings can have rights, and where man is free to rise to greater heights, are the aims of Scientology." Again, another religion that its whole predapiss is based on a utopia of peace and harmonization. Was this man escaping the bondage of bankruptcy like Joseph Smith? Is this a new outlook on the how the future will dissolve into? Is this a wrongful thought process, and how is it different than the other cultures of religion? Are we truly from another plane of existence? Can science be a part of religion?

This is a lot to take in, or by now you have discarded any notion of listening to this concept anymore. I have tried to ask you to keep an open mind on things. These religious factions do hold some part in the outcome of this I can assure you on this. Now, evolution takes on many forms, like I have previously stated. This one is more on a physical plane; the way of Charles Darwin had predicted. Now, the theory of evolution is not a religion in the matter of some deity, however like stated before if people believe in the same process and ways of teachings it is a religion by any accords. With this said, the world of true Science like the Charles Darwin the theory of evolution, Albert Einstein in the theory of string theory, Sir Isaac Newton in the gravitational forces, Michael Faraday's the theory of laws of magnetism,

Fritz Zwicky the theory of dark matter, and so on. These men are what we call scientist proving to the world how things work in our universe. Some can agree and others can disagree on these theories, however, the fact remains they show proof as well as ideas that take a little faith to which is known as theories, or hypotheses. How are they different than a prophet of some accord spreading the ideas of their faith? Does this mean that the science is truly a religion, and if so is it the world's largest one since the dawn of time?

The world of science has a beginning on how the universe was created and a revelation of the end of it all. The beginning is what is known as the Big Bang Theory, (and no not the T.V. show), which it states that during some time fourteen billion years ago there was a singularity which in layman's terms an immense explosion of energy that spread across the ever- expanding universe. From this, it created the stars, planetary alignments, and other unknowns that are out there. Though the world of mathematics, physics, and the undaunting to stride forward in knowledge to explain the how, why, where, when, and who we have come to exist today. They have also said, there will be an end to all of this as well, this is known as the Big Crunch if you will. This is merely studying the law of conservation of energy, which the laws of thermal dynamics are a part of. There are three main laws of thermal dynamics, the first law states: that energy cannot be created nor destroyed in an isolated system. The second law states: that entropy (lack of order or predictability; gradual decline into disorder) of any isolated system always increases. The third laws states: that when entropy is reach of an isolated system will approach a constant value of absolute zero. So, at some time in the future, all that energy that was produced will dissipate and there will be emptiness once again. I know what you are thinking he is a mad man, how dare he bring the notion that pure science infringes upon the borders of religion. I can assure you that this is not my intentions, but merely an observation. Is true science the lost tribe of religion, and are we to understand the meaning of life is through this way?

From time to time there are new religions that spring up giving a new idea, or concept of thought to the world of religion. Sometimes an old religion what you will call a revamping process or overhaul that they will go through, to pique the interest of their members, or something that is wrong and needs to be pointed out. In today's world religion has adapted to ways of times, some may say the ways of man. There has been a correction of error in religion, like people are not being tortured, burnt at the stake, and crucified in the town square anymore for heresy. Not since the days of Martin Luther, who was a pioneer on this matter rectifying the belief system of things that need to point out. There was another like Martin, he goes by the name of Charles Peter Wagner. His movement in the religion world is known as the Apostolic Reformation Movement. He had started this movement just like what Martin had done centuries ago, is pointing out facts that are wrong in the Church. Now, Charles was also a person of God in the ministry just like Martin Luther, and like all things new he also shares in the trials and tribulations like Martin had gone through, most likely not quite as harsh.

Since I have decided to come back to the fold, find my path to God, or what choice you prefer to call it, I told myself that one I was going to take more seriously, than I did when I was growing up, which means that I will read more, and do more. Seeing how my love of true science and the notion of common sense still are a part of me, and yes, I do have a hard time with faith and common sense if you will. The reason that I'm telling you, by whatever means people can call it either destiny, Gods will, or the laws of probabilities that I have found myself going to a church that believes in this movement. So, I have decided to interview the Apostle that preaches at this church that I go to. I am a very inquisitive person in matters of this faith, and wanting to know, not only how they operated as a church, but also how are they different from other faiths, and why the Holy Bible or scriptures say the things that they do.

During an interview that I had conducted, I have asked an Apostle of this faith, a series of serious questions. Apostle Wright also better known as Terrell Wright of the New Creation Apostolic Church in Hobbs New Mexico. What got him started in the ministry I asked, and like those to this world he said, "I was called to it". I go on asking questions like are you a cult of some kind and he replies "no". I go on asking him what is the Apostolic Reformation really about, his quote was "The return to original blueprint of Jesus Christ" and then I asked if he can elaborate on the subject matter for me. He was gracious enough to go more into detail with me by saying "It is the original intent of the Bible to make sure align the church up to the purpose that Gods calls for from internal into the natural". Then I ask the question how are you different from other Protestant or Catholicism altogether he goes on record saying, "That we are not set apart, because we are still the body of Christ, but being in part of the body of Christ that times God has transitions into the Church is what God is asking from the body, and God said I'm moving my body into the Apostolic Movement". The Apostolic Movement should have been the original church from the beginning, or better known as the Church of Jesus Christ he goes on saying.

The interview lasted about a half hour or so, and in the interview, I question what are some different things that the church is doing wrong that this movement is trying to rectify, and one example is how the church has governed its body. For example: in the Bible there are no Popes, Cardinals, Fathers, Bishops in the government of the church, however in the government of the church in accordance to the Bible Ephesians 4:11 it states that there are Apostles, Prophets, Evangelists, Pastors, and Teachers. Things of this nature is what the movement has to proclaim on the matters of the church and how it is preaching to the world. Is it good that religion is to be shaken up from time to time? Are we to believe in the ways that we grew up in? Is this the right path that we have to follow? Only time can tell on the matters of faith.

Chapter 9:

"The Final Piece of the Puzzle"

As we come into this world as an infant we have no understanding of the things that are around us, however at the same time having the knowledge of the universe. What do I mean by this you ask? In some cultures, such as the Tibetan Buddhist, it is in their belief that we are the reincarnation of our self. Let me explain, the Buddhist see life as a continuous cycle that repeats like an Ouroboros, until one has learned what one needs in order to attain enlightenment and enter into Nirvana. Basically, we are doomed to repeat life until we get it right. Keep this in mind as we progress forward into our journey.

When religion was used to explain how things operated in the world eons ago, it has manifested into something far greater than anyone could have hoped for. I have asked series of questions throughout this book, and sometimes I have answer them, however, I have not answered the underline tone to the main question, and that is, where is this journey that he is leading me to. Throughout time and incalculable tongues and camp fires, over rulers and dictators, prophets and Messiahs, holy scriptures to holy scriptures, there has been one message, and that is where did we come from.

As I previously stated in the beginning of this book that I might be a mad man trying to have one unified theory of belief in the ways of all religious aspect and not to mention science itself. This is how I have perceived it to be. Each faith talks about the path or the relationship back to the Holy One, kind of how Taoism is explained, in one form or another. Like I stated early that the Holy Bible is the key, however that key needs to be filed down in order to unlock the mysteries of the universe.

I quoted the first chapter of the book of Genesis, and the reason that I did this is because of the big three, Judaism, Catholicism and the Islamic faith share in the same beginning. I will be using the book of Genesis as my first stepping stone to allow you to see where I am coming from. So, with that being said; In the beginning, God created the heavens and earth as it states, now man, over time has tried to explain this part in religion, however from a science stand point it is said to be the Big Bang Theory. Which states at one point in time that there was a singularity that erupted, and energy was spread throughout the known universe. I think that both concepts are one in the same if you will. Faith is a way of belief and science is the way how man can unfold what God's plan is, which has been set for us in a certain epoch. My reason for this idea is this, God created everything in seven days, which leads me to believe that God's plan from start to finish was done in those days down to its most finite detail.

Which brings me to my next point with the book of Genesis, it states that this process was created in mere six days and having the seventh day as a day of rest, as some religious scholars have believed that those days were merely thousands of years old. However, science has dictated that it was in the billions of years thanks to a man by the name of Claire Patterson. You ask how did this man arrive at this measure in time; he did this by measuring the decay of radiation to lead (Pb) in certain elements. I believe that God has been speaking to us since the conception of man and our banishment from Eden, however our interpretation through the eons have been misconstrued, but not all the time, and this is based solely on our education on the matter.

I believe that God did create the universe and that there was a Big Bang to it all as science has suggested, however, I do believe that there is a conundrum, and that is this since matter cannot be created nor destroyed only the passing of energy from one form to another. When the Big Bang had happened, I do believe that God was that energy that created the everlasting universe, but here is where I have to disagree with some parts of the Big Bang Theory. At the core of every galaxy, there is a super black hole and the gravitational forces either give it the spiral arms like some we have seen or an oval cluster. You see a black hole is a sphere that funnels energy into the densest form where a tremendous amount of energy is released and that is including light itself, so during the explosion at that finite moment energy has to go somewhere. Now, since matter or energy cannot be created nor destroyed and can be transfer of it from one form to another, that the black hole is just that a transference of that energy either moving it to another part of our universe or like a three by five card on a Rolodex to an infinite parallel universe that we coexist in the same time frame.

My basis of my argument is this, in the Holy Bible, it mentions the word worlds in Hebrews 11:3, and why is it in a plural state what is the meaning behind this? A lot of scholars of the religious faction believe that it is talking about heaven, earth, and the underworld, however, why can't there be more. This goes to show my argument that we live in a multi universe realm, and the transference of energy throughout these systems is how God had created us. Like the eastern religions that I mentioned earlier, they show us how to study the art of meditation and how to become one with the universe, and not to mention that we live in a life cycle. What do you mean by this you ask? God has granted us free will, and base on that free will we make decisions, and from those decisions that we make the information is written down on those three by five cards for events to play out. The next card, let say that you went down the other rabbit hole instead of the one that you just have chosen on the previous card. The reason that I bring this up is simple. God has created the heaven and earth in six days, however, on the seventh day, God rested. So, this means all the events that man has to go through have been played out base on our free will, in infinite time lines and parallel universes.

On the fifth day in the book of Genesis, God said: "Let us make man in our image". The question that I have is this, if God is one entity what is with the word "us"? The religious scholars believe that the "us" is the trio effect of the holy trinity which God is, The Father, The Son, and The Holy Spirit. Since God is all three, this leads me to believe that God is the embodiment of energy itself. So, the question is now where did we come from? Are we apes like what Charles Darwin had theorized about evolution, or are we the manifestation of what God has created? I say we are both, we are the construct of God's work, however, when God said that we were created in his image, God did not say in what state that we were created in. I think that we have evolved from a primitive form of homo-sapiens, and we will continue to evolve throughout time. My reason is this, and even though that it is a small part of the human body it goes to my proof that we are not done evolving into our next skin. The part of the body that I'm talking about is known as the appendix, both doctors and sciences have said in the next couple of generations that we will no longer have the used of the appendix, and humans would adapt to this way. Once that has happened then that epoch will begin, and who knows what will be next. I believe that since we were created in God's image and if God is energy then our evolution will become energy itself.

Which brings me to my next point. When the Aryans first introduce the idea that God created man and woman, and there was a number of us, and the reason that the book of Genesis talks about Adam and Eve, is because they were the ones that had eaten the forbidden fruit which God told them not to do that. Pardon the pun but they were a couple of bad apples that had to ruin it for all of us. For you see, prior to Adam and Eve eating that proverbial fruit that man could talk to nature and the creatures of the earth, and not to mention that they had eternal life. We had the power of telekinesis at one point in time, so what you are telling us we have that ability to shape life in our image. I say yes, since science and doctors around the world say that we only use one-quarter of our brains that there is that possibility, and since I have stated before that we are not done evolving. Also, the Aryans suggested that there was more of us at the time, the evidence will go to show in the book of Genesis after Cane killed Abel, and Cane was banished into the wilderness, he came across a woman which he had children by. Which means that there was more than one gene pool that we all came from. So, you ask this question why are there so many races if God created us in his image. We were created by the supreme being, however again this is where evolution has taken place.

Adam and Eve had a third son, which he had produced offspring of his own, this goes to prove that the nation of man was far greater than that of Adam and Eve. There were two tribes that we know about in the Holy Bible one being from Cane and the other the third son of Adam and Eve which was known as Seth. As the population had grown, so did the ranks of evil in men. God had seen this coming, and ask a man by the name of Noah to build a boat. As I stated before another man by the name of Utnapishtim also had the same story. Since the first five books of the Bible were written by Moses and the story of Noah was one in the same of Utnapishtim, my reason is this. Moses, even though his background was from a Hebrew nation, however he was raised as an Egyptian, and when writing the book of Genesis, maybe Utnapishtim name did not translate well from ancient Mesopotamia to his understanding. So, Noah was his new name. Noah was to build this boat and allow the creatures of the world to come two by two. You ask why the creatures did not kill them or the other creatures on this boat? Well once again to unlock the ways of the universe, God had allowed Noah and his family to obtain the wisdom that Adam and Eve had, which was the ability to have power over creation, prior to them being banished out of the garden. So, the next question is this what part of the family did Noah come from Seth or Cane, and not either one then who? In accordance with the Bible, we are the descendants of Noah and his family, however, Utnapishtim story is very much similar to that of Noah, but instead of just his family, he had brought some other people aboard the boat.

I do believe in the Holy Bible is the key to the way, I also believe that Jesus was God as the part of the holy trinity. The Bible and other Holy Scriptures all preach the Governing Body of God's Word, which is peace, good will to your family and neighbors, to have a relationship with God, to use his/her way and have faith in him/her to seek God out. The knowledge from the tree that Adam and Eve had eaten from, God knew that it was going to happen and had planned for it, so science and education in the word of God is ok. My advice to you is this find the relationship with God and yourself first and far most. If the church doesn't agree, in what you believe in, so what, just go for the education and the word to help you better understand him/her, because one day that revelation that might come to you could be the piece of a puzzle that God has put before you.

As far as religion goes we are all the embodiment of God the spirit. God being of the spirit an entity that is a construct of energy itself, or energy is the construct of God. If you believe in your religion dear to your heart while holding true to God's government, as I stated before, then you know you cannot judge, create harm, or any other aberration of sin. If your holy text does not jive to your understanding do some research on the matter, because maybe you find the message of God in another Holy text. For example: as I stated before the Holy Bible the sixty-six books are the key, however, it's just not the key it is the main body of the puzzle.

So, use it as your base and if you have troubles then meditate on it like how eastern religions do. Use a collaboration of all Holy text, because there was a reason that God wanted his children to come together during the Crusades, however man's decision of his free will at the time was poor.

A church is a structure with walls, a roof, and an altar at the center of it. The people are the church, and what the people believe is religion, and from time to time religion loses its way and needs to be grounded, like how Martin Luther did with the Catholic Church, how now the Apostolic Reformation Movement is doing to whole nations of religion, and yes, the non- believers that don't believe in any religion at all, but still live an honest life, they are a part of God's plan to keep us grounded so we don't lose our way.

I believe when you study the world of religion that you need a committee of different backgrounds in order to keep everyone on the right path. I also believe that God has drop pieces of the puzzle in every major religion throughout time. I believe that once we have obtained the idea that we are all fighting in our faith whether or not if you believe, is trying to find Heaven, Nirvana, that state where you can wake up without a care, and just to lived life as God had attended to be, like when we lived in the garden of Eden.

CPSIA information can be obtained
at www.ICGtesting.com
Printed in the USA
LVHW041029300720
661936LV00003B/461